I0140439

WOMEN OF A CERTAIN AGE

*Part Three of
The Gabriels:
Election Year in the
Life of One Family*

Richard Nelson

BROADWAY PLAY PUBLISHING INC
224 E 62nd St, NY, NY 10065
www.broadwayplaypub.com
info@broadwayplaypub.com

WOMEN OF A CERTAIN AGE
© Copyright 2016 by Richard Nelson

All rights reserved. This work is fully protected under the copyright laws of the United States of America. No part of this publication may be photocopied, reproduced, stored in a retrieval system, or transmitted, in any form or by any means, electronic, mechanical, recording, or otherwise, without the prior permission of the publisher. Additional copies of this play are available from the publisher.

Written permission is required for live performance of any sort. This includes readings, cuttings, scenes, and excerpts. For amateur and stock performances, please contact Broadway Play Publishing Inc. For all other rights please contact Patrick Herold, I C M Partners (U S A), Rupert Lord, MLRep (U K).

Cover graphic compliments of The Public Theater

First printing: March 2017
I S B N: 978-0-88145-700-1

Book design: Marie Donovan
Typographic controls: Adobe InDesign
Typeface: Palatino
Printed and bound in the U S A

WOMEN OF A CERTAIN AGE was first produced by The Public Theater (Oskar Eustis, Artistic Director; Patrick Willingham, Executive Director), opening on 8 November 2016. The cast and creative contributors were:

MARY GABRIEL .... Maryann Plunkett
PATRICIA GABRIEL .... Roberta Maxwell
GEORGE GABRIEL .... Jay O Sanders
HANNAH GABRIEL .... Lynn Hawley
JOYCE GABRIEL .... Amy Warren
KARIN GABRIEL .... Meg Gibson

Director .... Richard Nelson
Scenic designers .... Susan Hilferty
& Jason Ardizzone-West
Costume designer .... Susan Hilferty
Lighting designer .... Jennifer Tipton
Sound designers .... Scott Lehrer & Will Pickens
Production stage manager .... Theresa Flanagan
Stage manager .... Jared Oberholtzer
Assistant director .... Sash Bischoff
Production assistant .... Joseph Fernandez
Stage management intern .... Jessica Edwards
Prop master .... Claire M Kavanah
Associate line producer .... Danny Sharron
Prop runner .... Shelly Vance

CHARACTERS & SETTING

[Thomas Gabriel, a novelist and playwright, died one year ago, at the age of 64.]

MARY GABRIEL, *61, Thomas' third wife, and widow, a retired doctor.*

PATRICIA GABRIEL, *82, Thomas' mother.*

GEORGE GABRIEL, *61, Thomas' brother, a piano teacher and cabinetmaker.*

HANNAH GABRIEL, *fifties, GEORGE's wife, and Thomas' sister-in-law, works odd-jobs.*

JOYCE GABRIEL, *fifties, Thomas' sister, an associate costume designer.*

KARIN GABRIEL, *fifties, Thomas' first wife, an actress and now teacher.*

Time: Tuesday, November 8, 2016

Election Day

5:00 P M to approximately 7:00 P M

Note: In the published versions of The Gabriel plays, I use a single quotation mark to notate when the character is paraphrasing, and double quotation marks when the character is actually reading from a source.

"…and something went—wiggle-wiggle."
The Cherry Orchard (1903 version)

for Oskar

WOMEN OF A CERTAIN AGE

(An empty room: the kitchen of the GABRIELs' house. South Street, Rhinebeck, New York.)

(Refrigerator, stove/oven [Electric], sink; large wooden and rustic table used as a kitchen counter [with a drawer for silverware] is set beside another smaller table making an 'L' shape; a bench is to one side, facing the tables [on the bench, a small basket full of correspondence, bills, and small notebooks]; a beaten-up armchair; upstage a small cupboard. Chairs and a bench set upside down on the tables.)

(Exits: upstage to the unseen dining room; down left to the mudroom, back porch and back yard; down right leads to the rest of the house—living room, the stairs to the bedrooms on the second floor, and to the front porch.)

(In the dark, Lucius' Until We Get There *plays through the main speakers.)*

(MARY, HANNAH, JOYCE, KARIN and GEORGE enter with trays full of kitchen objects. They will create the 'life of the kitchen,' which includes a box of old books and magazines, PATRICIA carries in a folded wheelchair, which she sets upstage by the sink.)

(Though the character PATRICIA is partially paralyzed by a recent stroke, in this 'set up' she walks in and takes her seat.)

(GEORGE leaves and the lights change, and music fades:)

1.

Five Women

(The women sit around the table; KARIN *peels potatoes.*
HANNAH *has just finished mixing cookie dough. She
and* MARY *look through the box of old children's books,
magazines, etc.* JOYCE *sits looking through a children's
cookbook: Betty Crocker's* Cook Book for Boys and Girls.
PATRICIA *is the center of the other women's attentions.)*

(These five women have been talking here for a while:)

PATRICIA: Who's there?

(All listen toward the mudroom.)

JOYCE: I don't hear anything, Mom.

*(*JOYCE *to* MARY, *who shakes her head.)*

HANNAH: What do you hear?

PATRICIA: I thought I heard a door close, Hannah.

JOYCE: *(To the others)* I didn't hear anything.

(Neither did the others.)

MARY: *(To* JOYCE*)* I didn't…

HANNAH: *(Shrugs)* The wind?

KARIN: I'm sure I closed the door…

MARY: Sometimes if it doesn't click…

JOYCE: *(To* PATRICIA*)* We didn't hear anything, Mom.
You want us to check?

MARY: Why don't I go and see… *(She heads off to the
mudroom.)*

JOYCE: *(Back to the book in hand, to* PATRICIA*)* So how
about—a 'Bunny Salad'? Remember us making that?

HANNAH: *(Mixing the dough)* What's a 'Bunny Salad',
Patricia? *(To* JOYCE*)* Show me.

JOYCE: *(As she shows* HANNAH*)* I do remember us making this...

HANNAH: Cute.

KARIN: Why is it called a bunny salad?

*(*MARY *returning:)*

MARY: No one's out there, Patricia.

JOYCE: You okay, Mom? No one's out there... *(To* KARIN*)* That's half of a sliced pear. See, sort of looks like a bunny lying down... *(Shows* KARIN*)*

KARIN: Whose cookbook was this...?

JOYCE: *(Pointing out where someone has written on the page)* 'George'.

PATRICIA: George wrote his name in everything, Joyce. I don't remember a Bunny Salad.

JOYCE: I do... *(Turns the page,)* 'Candle Salad.' I don't think we ever made that, Mom...

PATRICIA: I think we did, Joyce.

JOYCE: I don't think so. *(Reading)* 'Muffins.'

(Phone rings off.)

JOYCE: 'Applesauce.'

HANNAH: *(To* MARY*)* Phone...

*(*MARY *wipes her hands and goes to get it.)*

JOYCE: 'Cinderella Cake.' Too much work, and I don't think we ever made that either. *(Another)* 'Choo-Choo Salad...'

KARIN: What's that?

JOYCE: *(To* PATRICIA*)* So, Mom—who is it?

PATRICIA: What? Who's what, Joyce?

JOYCE: On the phone. Who's calling? You're almost always right.

PATRICIA: What?

HANNAH: You are. *(To* KARIN*)* She is. It's—

PATRICIA: What?

JOYCE: *(Over this)* your— 'amazing gift'…

HANNAH: Joyce.

JOYCE: I'm not making fun. Mom, you almost always know just as the phone rings—.

PATRICIA: Know what?

JOYCE: Who's calling. You know you can do that, don't you? You know that?

PATRICIA: I know.

JOYCE: Still I've never really tested you. I've wanted to.

PATRICIA: Why do you want to—?

JOYCE: I'm going to test you. Come on, Mom. Tell us. It's all right, Hannah.

HANNAH: I didn't say anything.

JOYCE: So—Mom, who just called?

PATRICIA: It's probably, I think…

JOYCE: Who?

PATRICIA: George, isn't it?

JOYCE: *(To the others, as fact:)* It's George. I'll bet she's right.

KARIN: *(Peeling, over this)* It could be for me.

PATRICIA: I don't know, Joyce.

JOYCE: Oh you know. I just don't know how you know, but you know. And it's spooky…

*(*MARY *returning:)*

MARY: It was George.

JOYCE: Yes! What did I tell you? Mom, you're amazing. You are just amazing.

KARIN: *(Same time to* HANNAH*)* She was right.

MARY: What—??

HANNAH: Patricia knew who was on the phone. *(She will cover the cookie dough with Saranwrap and put it in the refrigerator.)*

MARY: George got stuck in traffic in Westchester; he just got off the Taconic. He didn't want us to worry. And he says cook whatever we want, he doesn't care.

KARIN: Pat, you really know who's calling—?

JOYCE: *(Over this)* You've always done it. You haven't lost your touch, Mom.

PATRICIA: *(To* KARIN*)* I don't know.

HANNAH: *(To* MARY*)* And Paulie?

JOYCE: *(To* MARY*)* Did he say anything about Paulie?

MARY: No…

HANNAH: *(Looking in* PATRICIA's *mug, to* PATRICIA*)* Would you like more coffee…?

*(*PATRICIA *doesn't.)*

HANNAH: I sometimes know that it's Paulie calling. I just sense it sometimes.

MARY: You're his mother. Makes sense. That's not uncommon with mothers…

HANNAH: I'm not always right. *(About the coffee)* There's still some left. Anyone…?

(No one wants coffee. HANNAH *will pour herself some.)*

JOYCE: *(The book)* Mom, 'Raggedy Ann Salad…' Can we do this? We have to do this…

PATRICIA: What do we need for that?

MARY: Joyce, your mother had a very interesting—fascinating—dream just last night… [to Patricia] It was last night, right? It was last night. *(To* HANNAH*)* We should tell her…

HANNAH: We should. *(To* JOYCE*)* It's fascinating.

JOYCE: What dream, Mom?

MARY: *(To* PATRICIA*)* You told us about it just this morning. *(To* JOYCE*)* Before you got here. We think she dreamed it last night.

JOYCE: What??

MARY: *(To* PATRICIA*)* Remember telling me and Hannah? We came to pick you up to vote. But you were too tired. You remembered so many details. I never remember the details of my dreams…

HANNAH: Me neither.

KARIN: *(To* HANNAH, *about the peeled potatoes)* In quarters…?

*(*HANNAH *nods.)*

MARY: All about your new roommate…

JOYCE: You have a new roommate, Mom?

PATRICIA: I do.

MARY: You'll meet her.

HANNAH: *(Over this)* Just this week. We've met her. The roommate kept saying, 'I don't belong in assisted living…' She wasn't saying this to us. She was just saying it…

MARY: In your Mom's dream… *(To* PATRICIA*)* Remember? You described being in your bed—.

HANNAH: Your mother's bed is now the one by the window.

JOYCE: Is it?

MARY: And the roommate, she is taking care of you. She's told Patricia that that was now her—the roommate's—job.

JOYCE: To take care of Mom?

HANNAH: Yeh.

MARY: Like she's now Patricia's nurse. When suddenly—in the dream—Patricia has her back to the roommate, and she hears this woman—.

HANNAH: Gail.

MARY: 'Gail' says: 'Patty, I'm so sick and tired of taking care of you… So why don't you just get it over with, and jump out that window.'

JOYCE: (*Quietly*) What??

MARY: And Patricia turns to her and says…? Remember…?

PATRICIA: I remember.

MARY: You say: "Why are you saying this to me?" The roommate says back, "But I didn't say anything to you, Patty."

PATRICIA: "But I heard you say that to me, Gail."

MARY: "Did you see me say that?" Gail asks. In the dream. 'No. I didn't.' Am I telling it right?

(PATRICIA *nods.*)

MARY: Your mother hadn't seen her, because of course Gail was behind her. "Then next time, Patty, when you think I'm saying something, turn around and look for me." Patricia rolls over with her back to Gail again, maybe falls asleep?

HANNAH: And then it happens again…

(PATRICIA *nods.*)

MARY: She hears Gail say: "Patty, just kill yourself." Your Mom wants to explain that because of the stroke she can't get herself out of bed, and so starts to turn around to tell her this, but Gail shouts at her: "Don't look at me. Just jump."

PATRICIA: "I can't. I can't get out of bed…"

HANNAH: 'I've had a stroke,' she explains.

MARY: Patricia just lies there. Then after a little while… She turns and looks at Gail. And asks, 'why do you keep telling me that? Aren't you taking care of me?'

HANNAH: And Gail just says—'Did you see me say that, Patty?' She'd been told not to turn around. 'Then how do you know, Patty, it was me?'

(No one knows what to say.)

JOYCE: Does anyone in assisted living know about this?

MARY: Not yet… When we take her back tonight…

HANNAH: Your Mom's taking all these drugs now. She thinks they're what give her such dreams…

MARY: I'm sure Gail's taking all sorts of drugs too…

JOYCE: Gail wasn't there when she told you her dream.

MARY: She was there. Listening…
(At the sink, she will fill a large pot for the potatoes.)

JOYCE: *(With the cook book, back to)* So, Mom—let's do a 'Raggedy Ann Salad'?

HANNAH: What do we need for that?

JOYCE: *(Reads)* 'Canned peaches…' 'A cherry.'

HANNAH: We don't have any of that, *(To* MARY*)* do we?

JOYCE: *(Over this)* 'Raisins.' For the buttons and the eyes and the shoes.

MARY: *(To* HANNAH*)* I think we have raisins…

JOYCE: 'Yellow cheese' for the hair.

HANNAH: *(Over this)* Joyce, you're going to have to go back to Tops Friendly—

JOYCE: I don't want to go back there... *(To* PATRICIA*)* You all right? Mom... Mom... *(Sings)*
My Raggedy Ann is a very old doll
She lay in the attic for years.

KARIN: *(Over this to* HANNAH*)* What's this?

HANNAH: I don't know.

JOYCE: *(Over this)*
Hm, hum-hum, hum-hum-hum, my Raggedy Ann
With her legs doubled over her ears...
Mom knows where that's from...

PATRICIA: Do I?

JOYCE: Come on. You remember. My little record player with the carousel that turned as it played... My carousel record player. *(To* KARIN*)* She sold it at some garage sale. The second I left for college.

(Laughs)

PATRICIA: Why would I do that, Joyce?

JOYCE: I don't know. I'd love to know.

PATRICIA: I don't remember any such record player.

JOYCE: I think you do...

*(*MARY *will put the potatoes on the stove.)*

HANNAH: Shepherd's Pie and 'Paint Brush Cookies' that should be plenty....

MARY: That's enough. Agreed? Have we worked this out? We'll just do that.

(They agree.)

MARY: *(To* PATRICIA*)* I had a Raggedy Ann doll. I sewed it back together so many times—it looked like Frankenstein's monster. I used to operate on her...

KARIN: Pat. I have a question for you.

JOYCE: What?

KARIN: Today when I came back from teaching, and Joyce was here, she told me something—but I think she's just teasing me.

JOYCE: Oh that.

HANNAH: They don't tease. Do Gabriels tease?

MARY: *(To* HANNAH*)* Thomas...

HANNAH: *(The obvious)* George...

KARIN: *(Over this)* About some sort of 'family ghost'—over in the guest room, above the office, where I'm sleeping? The room I'm renting? Joyce said as a kid—.

JOYCE: And teenager.

KARIN:—she'd seen it a number of times. *(Smiles)* I don't believe her. But I thought I'd just ask. There isn't any ghost, is there? I think she's just pulling my leg. *(She looks to* JOYCE*)*

PATRICIA: In the guest room? A ghost?

KARIN: Yes.

PATRICIA: There's never been a ghost in that guest room, Joyce. You know better.

KARIN: *(Looks at* JOYCE*)* Thank you. *(Smiles)* I can't believe I even asked...I'm embarrassed to have brought it up. A ghost... *(Smiles)*

PATRICIA: It's the basement, Karin.

KARIN: What??

PATRICIA: In the unfinished basement of the office; below where you're staying. Haven't you been down there?

KARIN: I looked—. I opened the door, I didn't know where that door goes, so I looked...

PATRICIA: And you haven't heard anything?

KARIN: *(Hesitates)* Not really. No.
(Tries to laugh)

PATRICIA: You haven't heard any scratching? Or some 'rapping?' 'Digging' noise...?

KARIN: And if I had...?

PATRICIA: So you have?

KARIN: I know that we have moles—. *(To* HANNAH*)* Didn't you tell me George set a mouse trap and caught a mole? And it's just dirt down there. So I figure moles could—.

PATRICIA: *(Over the end of this)* I remember being over there once—when that was your father's office, Joyce. And cleaning up his stuff. He always left his coffee mugs... Just sitting in the sink. And I went down into the basement—we kept a few trunks down there. I can't remember what I was looking for. I'm down there. And the light goes out.
(Then)
Must have burnt out, I thought. So it's pitch dark. When suddenly my hand—felt wet. I couldn't see anything. It was completely dark. I hurried back to the top of the stairs, I thought maybe I'd cut myself; was this blood? And I turned on the switch and the light came on. It wasn't burnt out. It had just gone out... And my hand, I could see—it was completely wet... But just water. Nothing else was wet. Nothing dripping. Except on one step—a puddle... I closed the door to the basement. And then I heard... this [knock,

knock, knock], Karin, and—I told you there were only
a couple of trunks there, but I heard—it sounded like
chairs being thrown against the walls and smashed. A
whole room full of furniture being broken up... And a
voice...

(Then)

A voice... My god, what a sound...

HANNAH: *(To* KARIN*)* You know she's joking don't
you?

(She didn't, all except KARIN *start to laugh.)*

HANNAH: They tease...

PATRICIA: *(To* JOYCE, *over this)* Thank you for letting me
get that far.

HANNAH: *(Over the end of this)* The Gabriels, they tease.

(Lights fade.)

2.
A Garage Sale

(The same. A short time later)

*(*KARIN *and* JOYCE *look through the children's cookbook.*
MARY *will cut an onion and some garlic for the Shepherd's
Pie.)*

HANNAH: *(To* PATRICIA, *answering a question)* We've
found a lot of things—stuffed in the back of closets, in
the attic...

JOYCE: George said he found Dad's fiddle...

HANNAH: He's been playing it all week.

KARIN: Joyce, I hadn't realized George played the
violin as well as the piano.

PATRICIA: *(Explains everything)* Oh—he's a Gabriel.

MARY: *(To no one)* Thomas played the fiddle.

KARIN: I didn't know that... *(Having finished the onions, to MARY)* What else can I do?

MARY: Let me think... *(She goes and looks in the refrigerator.)*

JOYCE: *(Looking at the cookbook)* What about Jell-O? With cut-up fruit. Look.
(Shows a picture in the book)
When's the last time we had Jell-O? Mom, I'll bet you still have a box of Jell-O somewhere. From like a hundred years ago. It never goes bad, like the Twinkies you'd feed us...

MARY: *(Over the end of this)* There's no Jell-O. We don't eat Jell-O anymore. No one does...

JOYCE: *(Putting down the book)* I really wanted to make a 'Raggedy Ann Salad.' Shit. What are we going to do for a vegetable?

MARY: We have canned peas. Patricia likes them.

JOYCE: How can you eat those, Mom? You know they have like zero vitamins left...

HANNAH: *(Over this)* She likes them.

JOYCE: It's amazing we all survived our childhood...

PATRICIA: What? I couldn't hear...

JOYCE: You heard me, Mom.

HANNAH: *(Over the end of this)* Oh and we did a little scouting expedition this morning, Patricia. We all went to—here, you might be interested in this—
(Goes to pick up the big magazine from the bench)
—a garage sale on Livingston.

MARY: *(Explains to JOYCE)* Mrs Voorhees.

JOYCE: *(To PATRICIA)* Not me.

MARY: You weren't here yet. We went right after we voted.

(MARY *gets parsley out of the refrigerator [already washed],
and will bring it over to* KARIN *to chop.*)

KARIN: You bought stuff? I thought you were trying to
sell stuff.

HANNAH: For like twenty-five cents… Look at this.
September—1910. *Ladies Home Journal.*

PATRICIA: *(Making a joke)* I'm not that old.

JOYCE: You're not? Neither is Pam Voorhees.

HANNAH: Maybe it had been her mother's…?

JOYCE: A garage sale on a Tuesday??

HANNAH: *(After a look at* MARY, *corrects)* An estate
sale…

PATRICIA: Was Pam there?

HANNAH: No, she wasn't there.

JOYCE: *(Over this)* On a Tuesday. A garage sale…

HANNAH: It was a preview.

JOYCE: What did Paulie buy?

MARY: He stayed outside. He said everything smelled
moldy…

KARIN: *(To* MARY *about the parsley)* Chop?

(MARY *shows how small to chop it.*)

HANNAH: A few others brought stuff to sell too.
Barbara Apple had a whole clothes rack of her Uncle's
suits, jackets…shirts.

JOYCE: The actor.

KARIN: A good actor.

JOYCE: *(About the magazine)* Look at this… They made it
so big…

HANNAH: Almost giving stuff away. George was
like… *(Dumb voice)* "Oh my God, Hannah, look at all

these neat clothes." I had to say to him: you wear the same thing every day. You're never going to wear this actor's things... Sometimes he doesn't see himself...

JOYCE: *(Looking at the magazine)* I thought you wanted to get George to dress better. Make him 'feel better about himself'. You're always saying that.

MARY: She was saying that just last night.

HANNAH: Not with those clothes. That's not him. In one of the upstairs bedrooms—there's still wallpaper with pictures of cowboys.

MARY: Her son must be fifty years old now.

JOYCE: Joey was our age, Hannah... And still is... *(To MARY)* Was Joey there?

(MARY nods.)

HANNAH: I wonder if he still sleeps there when he visits. I almost asked him. Little cowboys with lassos... *(Then explaining about Tuesday)* He told me today's a preview just for the village... Before the weekenders get their hands on anything... He put a yard sale sign by the Town Hall. So we'd all see it when we went to vote.

MARY: The villagers...

JOYCE: You think they chose election day on purpose?

HANNAH: Only people from the town vote there. Only we would see it...

JOYCE: Good for him.

HANNAH: *(To PATRICIA)* We went to get some tips for our own sale...

PATRICIA: Did you get any?

HANNAH: Not much.

JOYCE: Here... *(Reads)* "The Girls Club. With One Idea: To Make Money." Maybe we should all read this...

HANNAH: I haven't had a chance to even look at that—

JOYCE: *(Reads)* "An open letter to the American Girl." That's us. You too, Mom... *(Reads)* "I want to talk straight and without mincing words. Has your mother ever said to you: If I could have had as much when I was your age as you have now I should have been the happiest girl in the world?"

MARY: You didn't say things like that to your children, Patricia, did you?

PATRICIA: Joyce?

(JOYCE mimes locking her mouth with a key:)

JOYCE: Tick a lock... *(Continues to reads)* "The chances are that when your mother was a girl she did have an overdose of self-denial and unsatisfied longing..."

KARIN: Pat is that how you felt growing up?

PATRICIA: My mother did. That's my mother to a T.

JOYCE: Want to say anything more, Mom?

(They wait for more, then:)

JOYCE: I guess that's all we're going to get...
(Reads) "Your mother had precious good times. She dressed simply... And when you came along—"
her children... "...the memory of her own girlhood heartaches stirred all her tender love of you and so she gave you whatever you wanted. She gave you clothes which her own judgment told her were not suited to you." We just had fights over my clothes, didn't we, Mom?

PATRICIA: I don't remember any fights, Joyce.

MARY: Who didn't fight with their Mom about clothes?

KARIN: I wore a lot of my mother's clothes.

JOYCE: *(Continues)* "Your mother gave you money, of whose value you had not the faintest conception." I'll skip this part…

PATRICIA: I'm interested in that, Joyce.

JOYCE: *(Continues to read)* "She gave you praise you hadn't earned."

HANNAH: Is that true, Patricia?

JOYCE: *(Before PATRICIA can answer)* Maybe. That's maybe true, Mom. I give you that. *(Reads)* "She gave you privileges which you just abused—"

PATRICIA: Oh that's true.

JOYCE: *(Reads)* "She gave you devotion that you accepted as a matter of course…"

HANNAH: Patricia?

KARIN: Pat? True?

(PATRICIA mimes locking her mouth with a key.)

PATRICIA: Tick a lock.

JOYCE: Maybe I didn't appreciate everything you did…

PATRICIA: *(Mimes again)* Tick a lock…

MARY: One of Thomas' students—when Thomas was teaching… He came home one day, *(As Thomas)* "Mary, this student said the most amazing thing today." This relates to that. The student said that her parents keep telling her they just want her to be *happy*. But she told Thomas, 'Don't my parents realize the pressure that puts on me?'
(At some point she gets a frying pan and begins to brown the onions.)

PATRICIA: I don't understand… What did her parents do wrong?

MARY: Pressuring her to be 'happy', Patricia.

PATRICIA: Why is that...?

JOYCE: Sometimes, Mom—. I know just what Thomas' student meant. Sometimes, it's— *(Searches for the word)* 'helpful' to think of 'being happy' as something that's not in our own control. There are *other* factors. So, if/ when we aren't happy, maybe then we won't feel so damn guilty about that. Like we've fucked up. Or have let others—our parents—down...
(Then)
(Back to the magazine) Here's an article for you, Karin—

KARIN: What's that?

JOYCE: *(Reads)* "How to Furnish My Entire Flat from Boxes."

KARIN: Save that! I'm going to need that! Can I see? Let me see...

(Laughter; JOYCE hands her the magazine.)

PATRICIA: *(Confused)* Why does Karin need—??

HANNAH: For her new apartment. *(To KARIN)* I still don't know how you're going to make that commute every day from Kingston...

KARIN: We'll see...

PATRICIA: *(Over the end of this)* I thought you were living in the guest room?

HANNAH: *(Continues)* To Hotchkiss.

MARY: *(Over this)* She is, Patricia... But she's moving on...
(She will brown ground beef with the onions.)

KARIN: *(To JOYCE)* Look: an ad for Jell-O.

JOYCE: *(Joking)* We should have had Jell-O...

KARIN: It looks good.

HANNAH: It always 'looks' good.

PATRICIA: My Mother was like those mothers in that magazine...

(They wait for more.)

JOYCE: Is that it? Why was she like them, Mom? Tell us.

PATRICIA: She never wore makeup in her whole life. I can still hear her voice... You are very lucky, Joyce. I could have been my mother.

(No one knows what to say, then:)

JOYCE: *(With the cookbook)* A picture of 'Raggedy Ann Salad'. In color...

HANNAH: Patricia, do you remember where we keep all those cookie cutters? You had whole boxes of all kinds of cookie cutters.

JOYCE: *(Turns page)* Hannah: They have a picture. 'Paint Brush Cookies...' Do you need a picture?

KARIN: *(Starting to stand)* I know where they are. I saw them the other day... Two boxes of cookie cutters, way in the back of the pantry...I was cleaning out stuff...I can get them. Should I get them?

HANNAH: Sure. Great.

KARIN: I'll get them then...
(She goes.)

HANNAH: Thanks, Karin... *(To MARY)* Karin knows where the cookie cutters are?

JOYCE: Is Karin wearing one of Thomas' shirts, Mary? I've been waiting to ask.

HANNAH: *(To JOYCE)* Mary gave it to her.

MARY: She's been helping to clean out Thomas' clothes closet. We've been going through stuff. It's dirty work. She only has nice clothes.
(She covers the frying pan.)

PATRICIA: Why was Pam having a garage sale? Has she died, Hannah?

(Then)

HANNAH: Last month… While you were in the hospital, Patricia…
(Then)
We'll need paint brushes. The littlest ones. Patricia, do you still—?

MARY: Where they've always been, the 'junk' cabinet in the living room. We haven't started on the living room yet.

PATRICIA: Pam's son was there?

HANNAH: *(Nodding)* Joey even asked after you, Patricia. He'd heard you'd been ill.

PATRICIA: Pam probably told him.

HANNAH: Probably. And he'd heard about your selling the house. *(To* JOYCE*)* He hasn't changed as much as a lot of men do…

JOYCE: That's good to hear.

MARY: You all right, Patricia?

JOYCE: When Joey Voorhees was something like eight… *(To* PATRICIA*)* See if you remember this, Mom. Joey was playing ball just across the street in the schoolyard. I think I was jumping rope. And two kids grabbed him, and started hitting him. And all of a sudden Mom you run out of our house, and across the street and you push those boys away. You take Joey inside, into the kitchen. *(Gestures: here)*. I found you both in the kitchen… You'd given him a piece of cake. Do you remember that?

(Then)

PATRICIA: No.

JOYCE: You don't? Come on, Mom, you need to remember the good things you do too.

(KARIN *interrupts with two plastic boxes—the cookie cutters.*)

HANNAH: I'll take those, Karin… *(Plastic boxes)*

MARY: What else do we need for the cookies?

HANNAH: *(Again)* Paint brushes…

KARIN: There are paint brushes in that cabinet in the living room… *(Points)*

HANNAH: Are there?

KARIN: The junk cabinet, I call it. Want me to get them? I can get them.

HANNAH: Sure. That would be big help, Karin… Thank you.

MARY: Thank you, Karin.

HANNAH: *(As KARIN goes off to the living room, calls)* They might need to be washed.

MARY: *(Calls)* You can use the downstairs bathroom sink…

(KARIN *is gone.*)

JOYCE: *(Continuing the conversation)* You've done a lot of good things. Nice things… You need to remember them too.

PATRICIA: I don't remember those things, Joyce.

JOYCE: Yes, you do. You're just being stubborn. *(After a look at MARY)* Mom, Mary's been finding all sorts of things. Cleaning out stuff.

PATRICIA: I know.

JOYCE: Mary told me on the phone about a box of letters…I don't think she's said anything…

MARY: To Patricia. No. Not yet.

(Then)

PATRICIA: Can I see some of those, Hannah? [cookie cutters) I want to pick mine before Joyce takes all the good ones…

(HANNAH *sets a box in front of* PATRICIA.)

JOYCE: A box, she found way in the back of your and Dad's bureau. And… And on the top of the box—she just showed it to me when I got here—you'd written: "Burn after I die." Well Mary decided not burn them, Mom, because you're not dead.

('Smiles' at her 'joke' then:)

HANNAH: Not just Mary. I agreed too. So did George.

JOYCE: Mary, Hannah, George have read them, Mom. I read them while Mary was picking you up…?

(PATRICIA *looks through one-by-one the cookie cutters.*)

JOYCE: They're all about your sister…

MARY: I was just cleaning out the bureau, Patricia…

PATRICIA: *(Looking at the cookie cutters)* I know the box, Mary.

JOYCE: All the letters are to you when you were a girl… How sorry everyone was when Ellie died. Nothing we read seemed like it needed to be burned… *(To* MARY*)* Did anything to you??

HANNAH: *(Answering)* No.

MARY: I'm sorry if I should have destroyed them, Patricia…

HANNAH: *(To* MARY*)* You need help?

MARY: Sure.

(HANNAH *and* MARY *find work to do; getting cans of tomato paste and broth for the Shepherd's Pie, etc.)*

JOYCE: I want to talk with you about this…

PATRICIA: What's 'this', Joyce?

JOYCE: Reading the letters, and seeing you as a girl of thirteen, and how people wrote to you... How your Dad wrote you. The fact that he wrote you; you were in the same house, weren't you? Or had you gone away? One of the addresses was away...

PATRICIA: I went to stay with my Aunt for a while.

JOYCE: I hadn't known that. How could I know that? Thirteen. Ellie was my aunt.

(PATRICIA *looks at* JOYCE.)

JOYCE: Of course I never met her. The photo you keep at the home; was when she got married, right? She's so beautiful in the photo. You once told me, I'll bet you've forgotten this, that she'd been your best friend.

PATRICIA: She was older.

JOYCE: *(To* MARY*)* What was her husband's—? George knew the name. *(To her mother)* George told me something really interesting on the phone. I don't think he's told you yet.

HANNAH: He hasn't.

JOYCE: He did some 'exploring' on the internet, right? Ellie's husband... He was a model for advertisements? Wasn't he?

PATRICIA: Yes, Joyce, he was.

JOYCE: A very handsome man. Very attractive. George even came across one of the advertisements he was in...

(PATRICIA *looks at* JOYCE.)

JOYCE: For hats... And he found out other very interesting things too. I think they're interesting. I think we all do.... The best man at Ellie's wedding...? *(Then)*

You want to know?

PATRICIA: What?

JOYCE: There had been this big scandal—someone even recently wrote about, made a play out of it. Some Harvard students way back were thrown out of school for being homosexuals. Being gay. George discovered that one of these students was Ellie's husband's best man, Mom. At their wedding. Do you know what I'm suggesting?

(They hear KARIN *returning with the paint brushes:)*

PATRICIA: *(About a cookie cutter)* Hannah, shooting star. I forgot we had one of them…

HANNAH: *(Stopping* KARIN*)* Karin…

*(*HANNAH *gestures and* KARIN *goes back out again into the living room.)*

JOYCE: Mom? I'll stop. Never mind… Want me to stop?

(Then PATRICIA *looks at* JOYCE.*)*

JOYCE: *(And she continues)* George speculates—and this does make a whole lot of sense to me, Mom. What if your sister—. What if she hadn't known that her husband was a gay man. He might have thought he needed— 'a cover'. That's what gay people had to do then. There's actually a name for this. The world made us do that then. So maybe—Ellie at the Christmas party she went to on that night? She was at a Christmas party, right?

PATRICIA: Yes.

JOYCE: And she sees something at this party that makes her realize her situation. She leaves her husband at the party—we know she did this. And goes back to their apartment… We know she did. But she leaves no note… What could she write? Mom?

PATRICIA: My sister was high strung.

JOYCE: What does that mean, Mom? Anyway, just suppose what I'm suggesting is what happened—just think what your big sister would have been going through. She was trapped.

(PATRICIA *looks at* JOYCE.)

JOYCE: She was nineteen. Nineteen. She couldn't tell her parents. Couldn't tell your mother. Grandma would have told her to— *(In a voice)* 'make the best of it, dear.' Right?

(PATRICIA *'laughs' to herself.)*

PATRICIA: I don't know.

JOYCE: Or 'you must be doing something wrong.' That's what she would have said. Right? Right?

PATRICIA: He—played sports.

JOYCE: Mom.

PATRICIA: He was a good swimmer…

JOYCE: You know better. It wasn't her fault. And—it wasn't your fault.

(PATRICIA *looks up.)*

PATRICIA: I never said…
(Stops herself)

JOYCE: What? You never said what? You didn't have to say…
(Then)
But I think that is what you thought. That it was your fault? I read these letters to this thirteen-year-old child, and everyone is saying, in their own way, the exact same thing—Patty, it's not your fault. Cousins, an Uncle, Grandma's friends, one of your teachers… It's not your fault, Patty. Or your mother's fault. Or Ellie's… Or her husband's…
(Then)

What can we say to make you believe that?

(Short pause)

PATRICIA: I don't know, Joyce.

(Then)

Who's making the paint for the cookies?

HANNAH: I will, Patricia. How many colors?

JOYCE: *(To MARY)* Karin can come back in... *(To PATRICIA)* Can't she?

(PATRICIA nods.)

MARY: *(Calls)* Karin!

(Gets up)

She can't hear me...

(She heads off.)

HANNAH: I think you have four colors of food coloring. And we can make more from that...

JOYCE: *(To PATRICIA)* You all right?

(Then)

(With the cookbook) Look, Mom, there's a 'letter' in the front from *Betty Crocker* herself. "Dear Boys and Girls, Cooking is an adventure. It's really easy to cook, once you know how. You'll be trying all sorts of things— even a supper for the family some night to give mother a holiday..."

PATRICIA: You know, there was no 'Betty Crocker', Joyce. They made her up.

JOYCE: I know, Mom...

(KARIN and MARY return.)

HANNAH: Sorry, Karin...

(Lights fade.)

3.
Paulie

(A short time later; the same)

(MARY, an old book in hand, and JOYCE, leaning over her. PATRICIA, having just heard a noise in the living room:)

MARY: That's just the front door, Patricia. It's just George… He's back from taking Paulie to his college…

HANNAH: *(To PATRICIA)* When he's ready, he'll come and join us.

JOYCE: Mary, she said, found this old songbook in the attic, Mom…

PATRICIA: Paulie was upset?

HANNAH: He was.

JOYCE: We told you.

HANNAH: It had to have been a shock. He grew up playing in this house. His Grandma's house. I'm sure he's calmed down by now. He'll get over it.

JOYCE: *(Showing her the book)* Sing For America. *(Shows her the 'signature')* 'George.'

MARY: I used to sing this to my dog, Cleo.

JOYCE: You used to sing that to me, Mom… Remember singing this? *My Old Dog Tray.*

PATRICIA: I do.

HANNAH: I never sang that to Paulie. I don't know it.

JOYCE: *(To PATRICIA)* You want to sing it with us?

HANNAH: You okay, Patricia?

MARY: *(To JOYCE)* Just the chorus?

MARY & JOYCE: *(The chorus:)*
Old dog Tray's ever faithful,
Grief cannot drive him away;

He's gentle, he is kind,
I'll never, never find,
A better friend than old dog Tray...

(Off from the living room GEORGE *has begun to play an old fiddle tune. They listen, then:)*

HANNAH: We found your father's old fiddle-tune book. It was in the attic too...George was thrilled. He said he'd forgotten half the tunes. So he's just been practicing. He broke a string yesterday. We found a whole package of strings in the case. *(Amazed)* Still good.

KARIN: May I see...?
(Takes the song book)

MARY: *(To* JOYCE*)* You know, there's research out now about how a child's brain isn't completely formed until his mid twenties...

JOYCE: I didn't know that. *(To* HANNAH*)* Did you?

HANNAH: She's told me. It's good to know.

MARY: And yet we expect them to...

JOYCE: To what?

HANNAH: To understand, Joyce,—complex, confusing things... *(Shrugs)* Loss... Life...

(When the potatoes are done; MARY *will take the pot to the sink and strain.)*

JOYCE: *(To* HANNAH*)* Kids, Hannah. I don't know how you do it.

KARIN: Me neither.

HANNAH: You do what you do. Paulie's a good guy.

MARY: He really is. Smart. I love having him around. I miss that.

HANNAH: Though sometimes... As you've seen today, Joyce.

JOYCE: (*Shrugs*) You should see some of the actors I deal with. That was nothing.

HANNAH: We knew he'd be upset.

MARY: You know kids when they go away to school they like everything to be exactly the same when they come home.

HANNAH: This is a bit more than that.

MARY: I know.

JOYCE: I'll bet there were times when I was a lot worse than Paulie was. Right, Mom?

PATRICIA: When, Joyce?

JOYCE: As a kid, Mom. I'm sure I said things to you and Dad too…I know I gave you some pretty rough times…

PATRICIA: Oh god, yes. Joyce, you really did… And you said things…

JOYCE: You don't have to say it like that. And I don't think I caused you any more trouble than Thomas or George… The things they did and said, and got away with.

PATRICIA: Joyce, you were so much worse than your brothers. Much much worse…

JOYCE: Are you joking? Is she joking?
(*She looks to* MARY.)
Mom, what are you talking about?

PATRICIA: I'm not saying you're like that anymore… Not that you're now perfect…

MARY: You all right there, Patricia, you need anything?

PATRICIA. I'm fine, thank you, dear.

MARY: Joyce you want to do the potatoes? You always do great mashed potatoes. Never a single lump.

JOYCE: I get out my aggressions... My frustrations.

HANNAH: *(Holds up a tiny cookie cutter, to distract her)* Look at this one, Patricia. What do you think that is?

JOYCE: That's a Christmas stocking, Mom.

MARY: A Christmas stocking... I love the little ones. I'm so glad you didn't throw those out.

JOYCE: Unlike my little record player carousel...

(Fiddle music continues off.)

(MARY will check on the frying pan and get out a large casserole dish.)

MARY: When Paulie got here this morning he really seemed excited. About voting.

HANNAH: His first time.

JOYCE: He's going to be scarred.

HANNAH: He *was* like a little kid, Joyce.

MARY: Nice to see that again.

HANNAH: He probably wouldn't have wanted you to see him like that, Joyce. Being an excited kid. 'How do I do it? I want to do it right, Mom.' 'Fill in the circles. Put it into the machine...' He couldn't stop smiling. You're his 'cool Aunt from New York City'. He wouldn't have wanted you to see that.

JOYCE: I was looking forward to calling him tonight, once the election results—. Knowing it was his first time. And we'd talk about how his vote counted. If it mattered in any race...

HANNAH: *(A race where his vote would count)* Teachout/ Faso...

MARY: A nice aunt thing to do...

JOYCE: They need to hear that. The kids. That it matters.

MARY: I think so too.

JOYCE: I won't bother him tonight. Maybe later in the week.

KARIN: *(Having turned a page in the song book)* Mary, you can't sell this in your garage sale… That's the idea, isn't it?

JOYCE: *(Over this)* Why not?

MARY: *(Over)* What? Why?

(Fiddle music has stopped.)

KARIN: Look at this picture. Look. A little white boy in black face…Jesus. It's racist. *(Reads the book's title)* 'Sing for America…' Incredible… *(Setting the book down)* This was in your attic…?

JOYCE: Throw it out.

MARY: Recycle it.

JOYCE: Mom, *that* you keep?

MARY: I'll put it out later with the newspapers. I'll rip out that page…

(As GEORGE enters:)

HANNAH: Hi.

GEORGE: Mom, you're looking good. How do you feel?

PATRICIA: How's Paulie?

HANNAH: *(Points to a sweater on the bench)* He left his favorite sweater.

GEORGE: He was in a hurry to get out of here…

HANNAH: We told your Mother.

PATRICIA: Why did you have to tell Paulie, George?

GEORGE: He needs to start taking out loans, Mom.

HANNAH: *(To PATRICIA)* We told you this.

GEORGE: He needs to sign things. He needed to know why.

HANNAH: We didn't want him to come home for Thanksgiving and just see a sign on the lawn.

GEORGE: We only waited til today so we could tell him in person.

MARY: *(To* GEORGE*)* You want anything? There's beer.

JOYCE: I'll get you a beer.

*(*GEORGE *doesn't want one.)*

PATRICIA: He was upset?

JOYCE: He's still a kid, Mom.

HANNAH: He's not a kid, Joyce.

GEORGE: Good to see you in your kitchen, Mom. We don't see that very often anymore…

PATRICIA: Tell me what he said, George?

GEORGE: In the car, Mom?
(He sits.)
In the car… Let's see. His exact words, Mom?
(Laughs)

JOYCE: What's funny?

GEORGE: What were our son's exact words to his father? Mom, I think they were something like: 'Dad, so you're just going to let them fuck Grandma over?'

HANNAH: What?

GEORGE: Sorry, Mom.

MARY: What does that mean?

JOYCE: *(Over this)* He said that to you?

HANNAH: What does he think we can do? Who's them?

MARY: He's upset.

GEORGE: After saying like nothing for a half an hour. Just staring out the window. Then: "Dad, you're just going to let them fuck Grandma over?" That's what I said too, Hannah: 'Who's them? Paulie? Who is them?

JOYCE: Where to begin?

GEORGE: (Smiles) Right. Right. Where to begin…
(Then)
I tried to explain that it's not going to help anything by getting angry. Getting angry will not help you, Mom. 'The best we can do, to hope for—is to make all this as painless as possible for Grandma.'

HANNAH: He must have understood that. He had to hear that.

GEORGE: He asked why we hadn't told him, Hannah. 'I'm a grown up now, Dad.'

HANNAH: Come on. We waited so we could tell him in person.

GEORGE: That's what I said to him.

HANNAH: (To JOYCE) He's been loving his school… He hasn't wanted to come home.

GEORGE: (Over this) I know. I know.

HANNAH: Today we got him home. To vote…
(Then)

JOYCE: (To GEORGE) He's a kid.

(As GEORGE goes to get himself a beer:)

GEORGE: He's not a kid, Joyce.

(Then)

MARY: (To JOYCE) You said you'd mash the potatoes…

KARIN: For what it's worth, the things some of my students say—and with so much confidence. So damn confident? Then the next day…something else.

GEORGE: So what's all this? What are you doing? I haven't seen these cookie cutters for years…

JOYCE: We're making dinner—and, George, everything, we all agreed, has to come out of that book…

HANNAH: *Betty Crocker's Cookbook for Boys and Girls.*

GEORGE: I remember that.

HANNAH: *(Lists:)* Shepherd's pie. Paintbrush cookies.

JOYCE: Mary and Hannah found that book in the attic….

MARY: And all that stuff… *(The piles of books on the table)*

JOYCE: We even thought of making Jell-O…

MARY: Remember Jell-O?

JOYCE: *(Over this)* You used to love your Jell-O… Or was that Thomas…?

GEORGE: I don't remember.

JOYCE: Raggedy Ann Salad.

GEORGE: *(Over this)* I don't understand. Why?

HANNAH: It was sort of Paulie's idea.

GEORGE: Paulie's…?

HANNAH: When he'd just got here this morning. Before we told him anything. You saw how happy he was.

MARY: He told us about a game his friends sometimes play at—

HANNAH: This is where we got the idea. From Paulie.

MARY: At dinner in the cafeteria: *(In a voice)* "If you knew it was your last meal, and you could have anything, what would you have?"

GEORGE: *(To HANNAH)* Why would they play that?

HANNAH: I don't know, George. Kids… It's an ice breaker, he said.

MARY: He said the responses always fell into two categories—those who want something 'extravagant', to indulge themselves, a fancy bottle of wine—.

JOYCE: Wine? He's eighteen.

HANNAH: Come on, Joyce.

MARY: —that costs god knows what—some meal from some expensive restaurant...

GEORGE: Is that what Paulie would want?

HANNAH: No.

MARY: (Over this) And the other category: those who want something that they remember having already had. So with a nice memory attached... A nostalgic thing I guess.

HANNAH: He wanted that, George.

KARIN: What are kids doing thinking about 'last meals'? I don't think I'd even be hungry... If I knew it was my last meal. I wouldn't be thinking about what to eat...

MARY: It's just a game, Karin. And Hannah and I had just found in the attic—*Betty Crocker's Cook Book for Boys and Girls.* So we all got the idea to make everything out—.

HANNAH: —of that. Paulie loved that. He had even agreed to stay for dinner, George. I hadn't told you. I was going to surprise you. And not only going to stay, but he was going to help us cook.

(Then)

GEORGE: Where was I?

HANNAH: We were in line to vote. Paulie, Mary and I. I think you were talking to someone.
(Then)

This could be maybe the last chance to have a dinner together here. All make a dinner together. In your house. This house.

GEORGE: You said that to Paulie?

HANNAH: No. No.

GEORGE: We had to tell him, Hannah. He's not a kid.

HANNAH: I know.

(Then)

GEORGE: So when will this fantastic dinner be ready?

JOYCE: Don't make fun, George.

MARY: Give us about an hour.

GEORGE: Then, Mom, I'm going to go play Dad's fiddle for a bit. I'm getting better. It's all coming back…
(He starts to leave.)

JOYCE: You sounded good.

HANNAH: George, while you were gone, the real estate agent for the house came by.

(This stops GEORGE.)

HANNAH: He just walked into the kitchen. Didn't even knock.

GEORGE: What did he want?

HANNAH: He took pictures. Can he do that? Just walk in?

GEORGE: He has keys.

MARY: He scared your mother.

GEORGE: I'm sorry, Mom.
(He goes.)

(Short pause)

KARIN: *(With the song book) Sing for America?* Recycle…?

MARY: Thanks, Karin.

(KARIN *goes to put the book on a pile of newspapers by the sink.*)

PATRICIA: Paulie's angry?

HANNAH: I think, more like disappointed, Patricia. In us. *(Sees* PATRICIA'*s face)* Not you. Not you. Just—in us.

(Lights fade.)

4.
Cutting an Apple

(A short time later)

(Off, GEORGE *plays through the basic fiddle tunes book.)*

*(*JOYCE *mashes the potatoes.* HANNAH *will get the dough from the refrigerator and roll it out. All listen to* KARIN, *who is in the middle of quoting from a 'monologue'; she directs this to* PATRICIA *and* JOYCE: *[the others having heard it last night]:)*

KARIN: Pat, then she says: *(Quoting:)* "Part of the problem with empathy, is that empathy doesn't do us anything. We've had lots of empathy, but we feel that for too long our leaders have used politics as the art of the possible... But the challenge now is to, practice politics as the art of making the impossible, possible..."

MARY: She was like twenty years old, Patricia. We don't see this side of Hillary now.

JOYCE: It must be there. Somewhere. Don't you think?

MARY: I don't see it.

HANNAH: *(Over this)* Wellesley...

MARY: She's twenty. Twenty-one. Karin did a lot of it for us last night.

KARIN: *(Quotes)* She said, "We are all of us, exploring a world that none of us understands, and attempting to create *within* that uncertainty."

JOYCE: *(To* MARY*)* That's true...

KARIN: "But there is the feeling that our prevailing culture, and its corporate life...'

HANNAH: 'Corporate life...' Hillary. Where is this Hillary? Come on...

KARIN: *(Continues)* "Corporate life which tragically includes, universities—"

MARY: Thomas would have really agreed with that....

KARIN: *(Over this)* "—is not a way of life for us."

MARY: Hillary Clinton, Patricia, at twenty-one.

JOYCE: *(Correcting her)* Rodham. Hillary Rodham.

KARIN: Here's something the kids at Vassar couldn't believe.

HANNAH: *(To* PATRICIA*)* She did her show last week at Vassar—.

KARIN: "Trust..." she said—

HANNAH: Listen to this.

KARIN: *(Quotes)* "Trust is the one word that when I asked my graduation class what it was they wanted me to say for *them* in my speech, everyone came up to me and said, 'Talk about trust.'"

(Then)

JOYCE: I wonder if she remembers that...

HANNAH: I wonder if when she looks back... Does she look back? Can she look back? What she thinks...

KARIN: Pat, I end my play with a poem that she also recited at her graduation.

"My entrance into the world of so-called social
  problems
Must be with quiet laughter, or not at all.
The Hollow Men of anger—and bitterness
Must be left to a bygone age."

MARY: "*Quiet laughter or not at all—.*" Karin said she
wanted to end her show hopeful.

KARIN: I think that's important. Especially this year.
Especially when there are kids…

JOYCE: "*Hollow men—?*

KARIN: "*—of anger and bitterness.*"

JOYCE: They've been left behind?

(HANNAH *looks through the cookie cutters.*)

HANNAH: *(To* PATRICIA*)* So you going to come with us?
(To KARIN*)* What time's your show?

PATRICIA: Where?

JOYCE: Who wants to be alone tonight?

HANNAH: At the theater society. The barn… We've
been there. We saw *Godspell* there. Are you going to
come with us? We're all going.

PATRICIA: I don't think—

MARY: Come on, Patricia. It's a special night.

HANNAH: If you get tired, we'll bring you back to the
'inn'.

KARIN: *(Answering* HANNAH*)* Nine? Around nine? I
don't think things are that tightly scheduled. I suppose
it depends on… How things go tonight.

HANNAH: Sure. We'll see.

KARIN: Sometime after the polls close. It's just
excerpts…. They want like twenty minutes…

JOYCE: I voted today for that Hillary. She must be in there. Somewhere in there... You think she's still in there?

MARY: Long lines in Brooklyn?

JOYCE: Very long. I got talking to the young woman in front of me. I said, 'pretty exciting, right.' She said, 'I just hope Hillary knows that my vote is 'not him.''

HANNAH: *(To KARIN)* You want to do any cookies? You want to choose a cookie cutter...?

KARIN: I should get ready soon.

MARY: And she's wearing your glasses, Patricia.

PATRICIA: *(Confused, touching her own glasses)* What? Why?

MARY: Not those. We're not taking away those.

HANNAH: We'll have fun... With us girls... Joyce is right—it's good to be together tonight. *(To JOYCE)* Karin's found some other neat stuff for her show... *(To KARIN)* What's that weird bit—?

JOYCE: What bit?

HANNAH: *(To KARIN)* About the collars...

MARY: Why is that weird?

HANNAH: She'll like that. It's about clothes.

KARIN: She says, "Instead of the closed collars I usually wear, I've been told to change my wardrobe to a more open-necked look. To convey, I'm told, more openness."

JOYCE: One of Bill's pollsters told her that. Do what the pollsters tell you—that'll make you seem human.

KARIN: Then she says, "But I just tell them, I get colds frequently, and I need to keep my neck warm to avoid them."

(Laughter)

JOYCE: Good for her.

MARY: Makes sense to me. Doesn't that make sense?

HANNAH: Hillary's just saying 'fuck you'. Sorry, Patricia.

MARY: *(Over this)* You think so?

JOYCE: She is definitely saying 'fuck you'. "Convey more openness..." A man definitely told her to do that...

KARIN: Maybe Bill...

MARY: 'Fuck you.' Where is that Hillary?

(They notice PATRICIA starting to nod off.)

JOYCE: Mary...

HANNAH: Patricia? You want to cut out some cookies? We've got plenty of dough... The Famous Paintbrush Cookies. Why don't we set up Patricia so she can... We're choosing cookie cutters... *(Continues about Hillary)* And I give her this: she never quits. I do like that...

MARY: I do too.

(As she puts an apron on PATRICIA:)

HANNAH: Patricia, Karin bought a pants suit.

PATRICIA: *(Confused)* Why??

JOYCE: *(Obviously)* For the show. To be Hillary.

PATRICIA: A pants suit...?

JOYCE: *(A joke)* I guess she couldn't fit into any of yours, Mom.

PATRICIA: I have a pants suit??

MARY: Joyce...

HANNAH: *(To* PATRICIA*)* We can hang around here until almost nine, and then all go together to see Karin's show. And if you get tired, or whatever, we'll take you right back to the 'inn'. It'll be fun. I don't want to think of you alone in your room on this election night.

JOYCE: She has her roommate.

PATRICIA: *(Reaching)* I'd like an apple, please.

JOYCE: You want an apple??

MARY: *(Same time)* You hungry, Patricia?

PATRICIA: I would like an apple.

HANNAH: *(Takes an apple)* Here. You want me to cut it into slices?

PATRICIA: *(Taking the apple)* I'll cut it.

MARY: Help her cut it.

HANNAH: Let me—

PATRICIA: I can cut it, Hannah.

*(*HANNAH *hesitates, then hands her a knife; and during the following,* PATRICIA*—with only one hand, because of the stroke, tries to cut the apple into two. This is very difficult to do, and even painful to watch. Once or twice it nearly gets away from her. This takes a lot of struggle.)*

(All watch this, though try not to show that they are watching:)

MARY: *(A joke, to* KARIN*)* You going to wear the pants suit on your date?

PATRICIA: *(Totally focused on the cutting of the apple)* What? What date?

HANNAH: Karin has a date, Patricia…

JOYCE: Be careful, Mom…

MARY: She's not eating with us. She's just been helping us out.

JOYCE: Hannah told me.

KARIN: *(To* PATRICIA*)* Just your family tonight…

(They try and not watch.)

PATRICIA: *(Cutting)* A date?

KARIN: It's not a real—.

MARY: He's taking you to Gigi's.

JOYCE: You sure you don't want some help, Mom??

MARY: *(Over this)* Sounds like a date to me.

KARIN: He's part of the Rhinebeck Theater Society; I think he just wants to thank me for the show. I'm not being paid. There might even be other people with us at the restaurant.

JOYCE: *(To* PATRICIA*)* Don't hurt yourself…

*(*JOYCE *looks to* MARY—*no one knows what to do.)*

HANNAH: It's a date. If she bought a dress.

KARIN: *(It was cheap, the dress)* At Marshall's…

MARY: *(Over the end of this)* She bought a new dress.

JOYCE: I got new jeans… *(To* PATRICIA*)* You want me to hold it? It keeps slipping…

*(*PATRICIA *ignores her.)*

MARY: *(To* JOYCE*)* What do you mean?

JOYCE: For voting. She gave everyone who promised to vote a new pair of jeans. My boss.

HANNAH: Isn't that patronizing?

JOYCE: She's rich. Welcome to my life, Hannah. If you went to Ohio to canvas? You got new boots… I came here instead.

HANNAH: How much did the jeans cost?

JOYCE: I don't know.

(They try not to watch.)

JOYCE: *(Nods to* KARIN*)* She's here like two months and she's got a date…

MARY: He's in real estate. The date…

PATRICIA: *(Trying to cut)* Is he selling my house?

JOYCE: No. They've gone with someone else for that.

PATRICIA: My children grew up in this house.

JOYCE: I'm one of your children. I know.
(She can't take it anymore:)
Let me cut that for you… Okay? It's hard with just one…hand. Give that to me.

*(*JOYCE *Slowly takes the knife out of* PATRICIA*'s hand.)*

MARY: *(To distract her)* Patricia, you want more coffee? You need anything?

*(*JOYCE *begins to slice the apple.)*

JOYCE: There… That's better, isn't it?

*(*PATRICIA *starts to try and take off the apron with one hand.)*

JOYCE: What, Mom? What are you doing?

HANNAH: *(Over this)* What do you need, Patricia?

MARY: Tell us what you need.

*(*PATRICIA *starts to stand.)*

JOYCE: Where are you going?

PATRICIA: I want to go home.

JOYCE: What do you mean?

HANNAH: *(Over this)* You are home, Patricia. This is your home.

(Looks to MARY*)*

MARY: Patricia, what's wrong?

PATRICIA: *(Quietly)* I'm sad…

MARY: You can't stand on that leg.

PATRICIA: *(Over)* Please, take me home, Mary. I don't want to come here anymore.

JOYCE: *(Over the end of this)* We're going to have dinner, Mom. We're making dinner—.

HANNAH: Joyce is here. She came for dinner.

MARY: *(Over this)* We're all going to eat in your dining room.

MARY: *(Comforting her, over this)* It's all right, Patricia. It's all right. Come on….

(Off fiddle music has stopped.)

JOYCE: *(Over this)* Get George. Karin, could you get George?

(KARIN hurries off.)

JOYCE: Tell him we need him…

PATRICIA: *(Over this)* Where's my wheelchair?

HANNAH: It's over by the sink.

PATRICIA: Where is it, Mary?

MARY: It's right over there… *(By the sink)* It's just folded up

JOYCE: It's— *(Shouts)* George!!

HANNAH: Joyce.

JOYCE: *(Points it out)* Your wheelchair's right there, Mom… It's just right there. Mary's got it.

(MARY has gotten the wheelchair and is unfolding it as GEORGE hurries in.)

HANNAH: *(To GEORGE)* Your mother wants to go home —.

GEORGE: Mom…? *(To JOYCE)* What's going on?

JOYCE: Nothing.

HANNAH: She said she's sad.

PATRICIA: *(Same time)* Please. Please, George… Take me home.

GEORGE: I thought you were going to have dinner with all of us. They're making a real nice dinner. Joyce is here.

HANNAH: *(Over the end of this)* You've been helping us, Patricia.

JOYCE: *(Over this, to* GEORGE*)* She doesn't want to be here.

PATRICIA: George…

GEORGE: I'm right here, Mom.

MARY: *(Bringing over the wheelchair, over this)* Maybe you need to go to the bathroom first, Patricia? You want to go to the bathroom before we go home?

JOYCE: George…

PATRICIA: I do.
(She nods and starts to try to get herself up.)

MARY: She needs to go to the bathroom. *(To* PATRICIA*)* Not by yourself.

JOYCE: Mom. Help her, George.

MARY: *(To* PATRICIA*)* You can't move that leg… Remember? Let George help you. You don't want to fall down. You don't want that. Do you?

*(*GEORGE *has gotten* PATRICIA *up.)*

HANNAH: Hold on to—.

JOYCE: What can I—? Let George…

GEORGE: Onto my neck, Mom. Hold on tight.

JOYCE: *(Without moving)* I want to help.

(As GEORGE *lifts* PATRICIA *into the wheelchair)*

GEORGE: *(Over this)* And I'm going to swing your…
We've done this many many times. There. Good. Good
work. Really good work…

*(*PATRICIA *is in the wheelchair.)*

GEORGE: You just got a little tired… *(To* MARY*)* I think
it's what she wants - the bathroom. Joyce, will you take
her?

MARY: I'll do that, Joyce. I can do that…

*(*MARY *and* PATRICIA *head off.)*

JOYCE: I can do it…

HANNAH: *(Suddenly)* George, has she been in her living
room since they picked up the piano?

GEORGE: We always come in through the back… Up
the ramp…

JOYCE: *(About all that has just happened)* Fuck…

HANNAH: I think she's been in there… She's seen. I'm
sure. Never mind…

(No one knows what to do or say.)

(Then:)

KARIN: I should get changed… *('Smiles')* For my
date…? You don't need me for…?

HANNAH: No. No, nothing. Thanks, Karin.

KARIN: You all okay?
(She heads off to the office.)

HANNAH: *(To* KARIN *as she goes)* I thought it wasn't
a date. *(To* GEORGE*)* Mary gave her one of Thomas'
shirts…

*(*GEORGE *shrugs.)*

HANNAH: Maybe Mary is going to need some help…
getting her off the toilet…?

JOYCE: *(Innocently)* She's a doctor…

GEORGE: I'll go see if she… needs help… And I can
drive Mom back to her inn… Sorry, Joyce.
(He is gone.)

JOYCE: *(Calls after)* And I'll go with you. *(To* HANNAH*)* I
have to leave early tomorrow…I want to make sure to
say goodbye…
(Then)
I really thought she was going to hurt herself with that
apple…I couldn't watch… She seems better though.
When I was up last month …

HANNAH: She'd just begun P T then. She's better.

JOYCE: I'm glad we're taking her back. She's tired. Oh
Mom…
(Laughs to herself)

HANNAH: What?

JOYCE: This afternoon, when I was reading the letters?
I was sitting in Mom and Dad's room. And while
I was lost, reading… I hear *(In a voice)* 'Hi.' A high
voice. *(Then)* 'Hi.' I look around—nobody there. 'Hi.'
It sounds like it's coming from Mom's closet. 'Mom?'
'Mom?' 'Hi.' And I'm about to go and look in the
closet, when I realize—it's just my stomach. *(Makes a
noise)* Sort of sounds like 'hi' doesn't it? *(Then)* Doesn't
it? You know how when your stomach is grumbling
and it sounds like it's—out there somewhere? Like
a thrown voice? 'Hi.' It was like that… It was my
stomach…

*(*JOYCE *sees* MARY *entering with* PATRICIA *in her
wheelchair.)*

JOYCE: Everything all right?

HANNAH: *(Same time)* That was fast.

JOYCE: You okay, Mom? I mean—.

MARY: *(Over the end of this)* False alarm. We're fine. Aren't we, Patricia? We're just fine.

JOYCE: I'm going with George, Mom, and take you home...

MARY: That's no longer necessary... Your Mother wants to stay. Don't you? How often do we have dinner with Joyce. Right? You want to stay with your family. You want to sit at the table? Stay in your chair—? *(Then, as an explanation)* She's wearing... *(Depends)* She forgot she was. She just got worried. It happens. No one likes to embarrass herself. *(To* PATRICIA*)* What about the chair there...? You sometimes like to sit in this beautiful chair.

PATRICIA: The chair...

MARY: Okay. It's more comfortable.

JOYCE: You're going to stay for dinner, Mom? That's great.

*(*GEORGE *has returned.)*

JOYCE: *(To* GEORGE*)* Mom's staying for dinner...

GEORGE: I know.

MARY: *(A joke, to* PATRICIA *about her new position on the armchair)* A change of scenery.

HANNAH: Let me help, Mary...

(As HANNAH *and* MARY *help* PATRICIA *into the armchair:)*

GEORGE: *(To* JOYCE*)* Dad's old chair...

JOYCE: I know. Good idea to move it into here. How much did you get for the desk?

GEORGE: Eight-five on eBay.

MARY: *(Helping* PATRICIA*)* I reminded Patricia what day today is. You'd forgotten.

PATRICIA: I did, Mary. I forgot...

MARY: Thomas would have wanted all of us to be here... He'd have been very upset... One year. One very long year.

HANNAH: How about a chair...? For your legs, Patricia.

*(*PATRICIA *doesn't want one.)*

JOYCE: What can I do?

MARY: Let me put a towel down... Under... Just a second... Could you get me a towel, Hannah? In the sink drawer... We'll use one of those.

(As HANNAH *gets a dish towel:)*

MARY: You just forgot, what today is... *(Explaining again)* Actually it was on the 9th, tomorrow; but Joyce has to get back... *(To* HANNAH*)* I'll hold her up... Put it under.

(As HANNAH *puts the towel under* PATRICIA*:)*

MARY: Now you can sit here in comfort and watch over us. You do like doing that don't you?

JOYCE: *(A joke)* And give advice, Mom... You love giving advice...

PATRICIA: Do I?

(As soon as PATRICIA *is comfortable:)*

MARY: What were we talking about?

(Lights fade.)

5.
The Buzzards

(A short time later.)

*(*GEORGE *sits on the bench.* PATRICIA *sits in the armchair, watching the others.)*

*(*HANNAH *makes the base for the cookie paints;* JOYCE *chooses cookie cutters.)*

MARY: I was in the Kingston Mall—.

JOYCE: I always hated—

MARY: *(Over this)*—the other day. What a depressing place that's become…

HANNAH: *(To* JOYCE*)* You used to like it. We used to go together.

JOYCE: As kids.

MARY: Half the stores are closed.

*(*PATRICIA *shifts in her seat.)*

GEORGE: You all right, Mom?

PATRICIA: I'm enjoying watching these girls work.

HANNAH: *(To* JOYCE*)* I think she means us.

MARY: *(Continues)* And—I was in that big shoe store, what's it called? I was the only person in there. And I am sitting and then I look up and there's this mirror on a pillar…
(She hesitates.)

HANNAH: What?

MARY: For some reason I wasn't—prepared…
(Shrugs)
I had my makeup on. Maybe I put it on a little too quickly… The light in our upstairs bathroom—you need natural light… And I'd certainly looked hard at myself before. To see what more will need to be done?

Do I start coloring my hair? I think now it's a bit late for that.

JOYCE: Hillary still colors her hair.

MARY: But to *start* now…? Who wants those questions? Still I'd never been *surprised* like I now was. Startled. I look up and it isn't just—oh there's something new, another—whatever to be covered. But what I see is a stranger… Do I want to know that person?
(As if looking at herself in a mirror)
Who is there?
(Remembers something and smiles.)

HANNAH: What?

MARY: Thomas used to say that one day he wanted to write a play with that opening line. The greatest opening line of all time of any play, he said.

GEORGE: What line?

JOYCE: *(Obviously)* Hamlet. "Who's there?"

MARY: That's how every play should begin, he said. "Who's there?"
(Shrugs)
I didn't understand.
(She will go and look in the refrigerator for tomatoes for a salad.)

JOYCE: Mom you are going to live to be a hundred and five. And I think that's really good. Means I've got those genes.

HANNAH: *(To MARY)* Could you get me another egg, Mary? For the paint.

JOYCE: *(Over this, to GEORGE)* You too…

(MARY will prepare a simple salad.)

MARY: I read somewhere—some book about dealing with a loved one's death.

(They are all interested.)

MARY: *(Checking the tomatoes)* I already washed these...
(Continues) How it was the custom, years and years
ago, in a lot of places in America—in the home where
there'd been a death, to drape black curtains over all
the mirrors...

HANNAH: Why?

*(HANNAH mixes the egg yolks for the paint. JOYCE will then
make the colors from this food coloring.)*

MARY: I just remembered this. *And* over any paintings
or photographs of landscapes... Landscapes.
(Answering HANNAH) So that the soul, as it left the
body, would not be distracted by a reflection of itself.
Or by a last look at the world now being lost.

I think it was out West... In log cabins...

GEORGE: *(As a joke)* You probably saw all that as a kid,
Mom...

PATRICIA: I don't think so.

JOYCE: My boss? In her office in the shop, she keeps a
print of Titian's *Venus.* You know, the one where she's
a plump girl, lying on the bed, naked, proud of herself
and her sexiness... She says it's her inspiration—and
her solace, and joy...

GEORGE: Is your boss—chubby?
(He joins the women at the table.)

JOYCE: No, she's very thin... But maybe that's how she
sees herself...

GEORGE: I don't understand...

(None of the women want to explain this to GEORGE.)

HANNAH: *(To GEORGE)* You going to paint some
cookies?

JOYCE: You and Thomas always liked to paint the cookies.

MARY: Did they, Patricia?

PATRICIA: I don't remember. Maybe.

JOYCE: *(To* GEORGE, *with the cookie cutters)* What do you want to do? A—duck? Here's a duck. Or a fish…?

HANNAH: Let him pick his own cookie cutters—.

JOYCE: *(Over this, with a cookie cutter)* What's this supposed to be? You know what this is, Mom? *(Shows her)*
I think it's supposed to be a squirrel.

PATRICIA: That's Santa Claus with his sack.

JOYCE: I think it's a squirrel, Mom.

(As they work: MARY *on the salad;* JOYCE *on the paint;* HANNAH *begins cutting out the cookie shapes:)*

MARY: *(To* HANNAH*)* Paulie didn't seem bothered about having to take out loans… That didn't seem to be what really upset him.

HANNAH: No. I don't think it was. *(To* GEORGE*)* Did he say anything about the loans on your car ride? Did you bring it up?

GEORGE: I did. He said, "What the fuck, Dad, I'll just default. Fuck 'em."

HANNAH: Fuck who? Who does he think is out there to fuck for having to take out loans?

JOYCE: *('A joke')* You mean, where do you start?

GEORGE: *(Smiling)* Maybe that's what he means. Maybe, Hannah.

HANNAH: *(Smiling)* 'Fuck them.' Maybe… Sorry, Patricia. Good luck, Paulie. Go ahead and try… See how far *you* get.

(Then)

George, tell your sister what you wrote under that guy's desk…

JOYCE: What desk—?

HANNAH: He built a small desk for a client—what does he do?

GEORGE: *(Shrugs)* A financial guy.

HANNAH: For his home.

GEORGE: He has a 'home office'. In his 'weekend' house. Some scam to get a tax deduction, I'm sure. I used to think there were *rules*. To them it's just a game…

JOYCE: What about this desk?

HANNAH: George wrote underneath…. You know so, say this guy drops his 'Mont Blanc pen', and has to crawl under to get it, and then he happens to look up… What will he see? What did you write? It's a quote. He knows it by heart. Tell her…

GEORGE: *(Quotes)* "I speak not the triumph of the sword, nor the wonders of science, nor of grandiose economic achievement, but only of the brotherhood of man."

JOYCE: *(Confused)* That's what you wrote? All that? That's a lot to write underneath a desk.

HANNAH: It's from the grave of a famous poet—.

JOYCE: And what does it mean??

HANNAH: It's obvious what it means.

GEORGE: I'm not saying it's going to change anything, Joyce.

JOYCE: What could it change? You scribbled that underneath—?

GEORGE: It's not scribbled.

HANNAH: I thought it was a pretty cool thing to do.

GEORGE: It made me feel good.

HANNAH: He wrote it in pen, Joyce.

(KARIN *enters in a dress; carrying the manuscript for her show.*)

JOYCE: All dressed up.

MARY: Look at you.

KARIN: *(Over this)* Don't tease—.

JOYCE: I'm not teasing.

KARIN: It's not a date.

PATRICIA: She's teasing.

JOYCE: You look—great. Doesn't she look great?

KARIN: Is it too—?

MARY: Karin, you really look good.

HANNAH: You do.

MARY: *(Over this)* It really fits great. And I for one can't believe she got that at Marshalls… *(To the others)* I can never find anything there… Did you want to wear my— *(Earrings)*?

KARIN: These are fine. What's wrong with them? And it's not really a date.

GEORGE: *(To* JOYCE*)* Mary was asked out on a date…

HANNAH: She doesn't want you to—.

JOYCE: *(To* MARY*)* What are you talking about?

MARY: *(Same time)* Come on. Stop it. I didn't go.

HANNAH: *(Over to* GEORGE*)* She doesn't want to talk about that.

JOYCE: Who was he?

MARY: Please don't talk about me.

JOYCE: *(Over this)* That's a good thing, isn't it?

MARY: Shut up.

JOYCE: A year's a long time. And taking care of him for years—.

GEORGE: I agree.

MARY: Shut up.

PATRICIA: *(To* KARIN*)* Put an apron on over that…

KARIN: I'm just –[waiting]

JOYCE: *(Pointing out an apron)* There's one on the…

*(*KARIN *looks at her watch.)*

JOYCE: What time is he…?

KARIN: Any time. It's not a date.

GEORGE: Hannah, Paulie also said in the car…

(All are interested.)

GEORGE: "Uncle Thomas would have fought all this…"

JOYCE: What's 'all this?' The mortgage—?

GEORGE: *(Over the end of this)* I guess, everything.

HANNAH: *(Over this)* How? How would he? Mary?

MARY: I don't know.

GEORGE: I think Paulie said it to hurt me. He misses his Uncle too. We've watched this, haven't we, Hannah?

HANNAH: We have.

GEORGE: We've tried to talk to him about it. And we all know Thomas would not have known how to fight anymore than we do. Or who…

MARY: No. I don't think he would.

JOYCE: No.

GEORGE: I started thinking, driving back— remembering, it just popped back into my head. When

Thomas had just gone off to college. And how that was really hard on me. I felt such an incredible loss. My big brother gone. I didn't tell anyone I felt that. *(To* JOYCE*)* You were too young. *(Continues)* And finally he came home at Thanksgiving, and he didn't seem all that different. And he still seemed interested in me, spent time with me. He told me about school. And, Mom, do you remember how he and Dad fought at dinner? They really fought: 'We're going to make things better, Dad!'

MARY: Thomas said that?

GEORGE: 'More just.' 'Well you just do your homework, Tommy." Dad. "And never sign your name on any kind of petition, Tommy. Never." He was always afraid of that. Really worried about us doing that. "You're there to get an education. Period. That's why you're in college." Remember?

PATRICIA: I do…

GEORGE: Thomas looked at me across the table, winked at me, and I knew what he was thinking: 'Little brother, look at how scared our father is.'
(Then)
Thomas was exactly Paulie's age… And Dad was mine…

(Then)

HANNAH: George and Paulie had a big fight over Bernie this summer.

GEORGE: Bernie's looking better ever day, Hannah. Maybe the only one who is…

HANNAH: You need to say that to Paulie.
(Then)
Mary, you want to know what Paulie shouted at George when they were fighting about Bernie?

GEORGE: What?

HANNAH: 'Dad, what about us?'

GEORGE: He did.

JOYCE: *(To* MARY*)* Thomas would always—.

MARY: We know. We all know that.

HANNAH: 'What about us?' Just like Thomas.

PATRICIA: Your father only wanted you to not make a mistake that you'd later regret. He always said he only wanted you children to be happy…

JOYCE: Happy, Mom? Do you remember what Mary was telling us about Thomas' student?

PATRICIA: I heard.

GEORGE: What? That's all we want too for Paulie, isn't it, Hannah? That's what we say. 'Just be happy.'

PATRICIA: I always wanted more than that for you.

(Then)

MARY: Hannah's now working as a maid, Joyce.

JOYCE: What?? What are you talking about?

MARY: *(Over this)* They haven't told Paulie. You didn't know that. I thought you didn't know.

HANNAH: Just part time—.

MARY: At the Rhinecliff Hotel.

HANNAH: We're not 'hiding' it, Mary.

GEORGE: We just haven't told him yet.

JOYCE: When did this start?

HANNAH: We need the money. The catering has slowed, who gets married in November?

MARY: She makes the beds. Cleans the rooms. Cleans the bathrooms. You told me you're the only maid there who speaks English. So she's started helping the other maids. On your breaks, right? With their English. Good for you. That's a good thing to do.

HANNAH: Thank you.

JOYCE: I didn't know.

GEORGE: Just until Mom can come and live with us. 'Assisted living' is even more expensive...

HANNAH: *(To* PATRICIA*)* You are getting so much better, Patricia... *(To* JOYCE*)* Every day. We're taking things one month at a time. We're 'working' through our savings...

MARY: Paulie's 'fund'...

(Then)

GEORGE: You know what's funny, Joyce?

JOYCE: What? What is funny?

GEORGE: Less than two miles from the Rhinecliff Hotel is the Astor estate. And Joyce, our grandmother—Dad's mother—she was a maid there, for the Astors...

JOYCE: I know that.

GEORGE: *(Over this)* So I've been kidding Hannah that it's like we've gone back in time... Gone backwards...

JOYCE: I don't think you should tease her about that.

HANNAH: *(Trying to make a joke)* I've got like the same damn job now as your grandmother...

(GEORGE *will hand out the parchment paper sheets for the cookies.)*

JOYCE: So Mom, you are going to move in with Hannah and George. I didn't know that was completely decided.

HANNAH: When she's ready.

GEORGE: *(Same time)* When she can.

HANNAH: Her bedroom will be the living room. Because of the stairs...

JOYCE: *(To* HANNAH*)* Don't you need a living room?

HANNAH: I have a kitchen...

(Off doorbell)

JOYCE: Karin, there's your date.

KARIN: *(Getting up)* It's not a date.

*(*JOYCE *is getting up.)*

KARIN: What are you doing?

JOYCE: I'm going to answer the door.

KARIN: No.

MARY: *(Over this)* I'll go with you.

KARIN: *(Over this)* I can answer the door myself.

JOYCE: I don't think that's right... Is that right? Should she answer the door?

(Chorus of 'no!')

JOYCE: Wait...

(Fixes KARIN'*s collar)*

KARIN: *(Over this)* Come on.

JOYCE: That's better.

(Another doorbell)

JOYCE: *(Teasing)* Oh he's eager... Come on.

(The three are on their way out.)

PATRICIA: Order something really expensive.

KARIN: I will.

JOYCE: *(Suddenly worried)* Karin...
(Stops her)
You have 'protection'? *(Her joke)*

KARIN: Oh fuck off…

(JOYCE, MARY, KARIN *are gone.*)

PATRICIA: Joyce teases too much…

HANNAH: *(To* GEORGE*)* I am going to call Paulie tonight.

GEORGE: He's not going to answer, Hannah. He doesn't want to talk to us.

HANNAH: Then I'll call his roommate. I have that number.

GEORGE: How did you get that?

HANNAH: When we moved him in. The mothers exchanged phone numbers. Mother's do that. Just in case, we said. Please, don't try and talk me out of it. Please…

PATRICIA: George, do you remember your Grandmother and the mashed potatoes?

GEORGE: No, Mom. No. I don't.

PATRICIA: She'd have to clean out the cracks in their dining room table—

HANNAH: Who?

PATRICIA: The Astors. Clean out mashed potatoes with a knife. They'd let their kids shove them in the cracks. She said she overheard once someone saying, pointing to her, 'that maid will clean it up…'

(*As* MARY *and* JOYCE *return:*)

JOYCE: *(Entering)* He had his nose pressed against the window…

HANNAH: Did you meet him?
(*She moves the cookies onto plates.*)

MARY: She wouldn't let us.

JOYCE: *(Over this, to* MARY*)* I think she bruised my arm. *(To the others)* Like in one second, she was right out the door—.

MARY: *(To* JOYCE*)* He looks like a real estate agent.

JOYCE: That's what I thought. *(To* HANNAH*)* Let me do that.

GEORGE: Isn't that what he is?

MARY: Yeh. But he also looks like one. I think I've seen him around.

(As GEORGE, HANNAH *and* JOYCE *set themselves to paint, cut-out cookies passed around, etc.)*

HANNAH: And, Joyce, you probably don't know this either. About Mary…
(She looks at MARY.*)*

JOYCE: What?

HANNAH: Mary can't renew her doctor's license. And it's not just a few tests. She'd have to take everything all over again.

MARY: I can't do that, I'm too old. I was stupid.

HANNAH: So Mary's thinking of being a substitute science teacher over in Ulster.

MARY: They need them. And if you don't have a teacher's license you can still substitute up to 16 weeks in the district. So I figure, I'll sign up in three or four districts. I should be able to get enough work.

JOYCE: *(To* GEORGE*)* Did you know that?

*(*GEORGE *nods.)*

JOYCE: In Ulster? Kingston?

MARY: And my daughter's very clear now she doesn't want me in Pittsburgh.

HANNAH: She hasn't actually said, Mary…

MARY: She's 'said', Hannah. I think it's her father she doesn't want to upset... They are close.

JOYCE: *(To* HANNAH*)* When did this happen?

HANNAH: Her daughter called last night...

*(*MARY *smiles.)*

JOYCE: What?

MARY: It's like *she* discovered Hillary! Like until about two months ago she'd have nothing to do with her. *(As her daughter)* 'I'll never trust her...' Now she's calling 'making sure' I vote today. 'It really matters, Mom. She came to Pittsburgh today, Mom! I saw her in person. We can't let him win. And remember she's a woman.'

HANNAH: I think we already knew that.

GEORGE: She's in Pennsylvania. So that's good...

JOYCE: Kingston? You're moving there?

*(*MARY *shrugs.)*

HANNAH: Mary, tell Joyce about the lawyers' office in Kingston—.

MARY: You tell her.

JOYCE: *(Over this)* What?

HANNAH: There's a law office—.

GEORGE: Two houses down from where Karin's new apartment is—.

MARY: We all went to look at Karin's new apartment. You went with us too, Patricia, remember?

HANNAH: It's called 'Rounds and Rounds: Attorneys at Law.' Rounds and Rounds—we go...

GEORGE: 'We've got you coming and going.'

MARY: 'And we'll take forever doing it!'

(Laughter)

GEORGE: Out of Dickens… Like us.

(Laughs)

HANNAH: *(Over this)* It is. You're right… We are. He's right…

(MARY *works on the salad.*)

JOYCE: We could all start a NORC…

PATRICIA: What's that?

JOYCE: We could take care of each other. Grownups. Who needs kids?

MARY: A NORC, Patricia, a community of people of a certain age *(Like us)* who take care of each other. Live together…

JOYCE: *(Painting)* When I was in Paris-

HANNAH: Oh 'Paris', 'I go to Paris'.

JOYCE: Shut up. This is an entirely different subject. I visited this famous cemetery there.

GEORGE: A NORC, a cemetery. Is this really a new subject?

JOYCE: *(Continues over this)* A huge place. Like a city itself. Lots of famous people—Oscar Wilde. Lots. A crematory where the ashes are put into a wall in like little slots. Isadora Duncan is there. *(Smiles)* She's just called 'Dora Duncan.' I guess her whole name didn't fit. There was a workman there, cleaning out a slot. I learned later that these 'slots' are just rented and so when… Then—you're forgotten… Thrown away? I don't know. He's cleaning out the 'slot' and there's another empty slot just above, and he puts his plastic bottle of apple juice in there. I'm looking and there are all these names and then this plastic bottle of apple juice… Taking up its own slot… Why do I keep remembering that?

HANNAH: *(Painting)* NORCs. Cemeteries. When do we start talking about our illnesses? Come on, we're fucking Gabriels.

PATRICIA: What does that mean?

GEORGE: I don't know, Mom… Anyone know?

(KARIN returns, still with her script.)

MARY: Karin? Why are you back?

HANNAH: *(Over this)* You okay?

KARIN: He uh…

GEORGE: What? He what?

JOYCE: Where is he?

KARIN: He's—gone to dinner. I want a beer.

(GEORGE starts to get up.)

KARIN: I can get it…

(GEORGE goes to get a beer from the refrigerator.)

KARIN: We got as far as the traffic light. We're waiting for the WALK sign… Sometimes that seems to take forever.

HANNAH: It can…

KARIN: *(Taking the beer)* Thank you.

MARY: You want a glass? She wants a glass.

KARIN: I do. I like a glass.

(MARY goes to the sink, gets KARIN a glass.)

KARIN: He asked if later he could see upstairs. Your second floor. For a minute, a very stupid minute, I thought he—you know—thought that I was sleeping up there. So I said—I'm staying in the office, in back, upstairs *there*. He said, he'd probably like to look at that too.

JOYCE: I don't understand.

KARIN: But the upstairs here really interested him. How big are the bedrooms…? The square footage. He had a tape measure with him.

HANNAH: What??

KARIN: *(Taking the glass)* Thank you. The second we left *(Snaps her fingers)* he started asking about the house. Leaks? The basement. We're walking down the street, and it's all he will talk about. How—when it's listed this week, it could still be listed with him too. They do that. 'We can do that.' He has someone interested. I ask him, are we only going to talk about the house? And he said—is that all right?
(Sips her beer)

HANNAH: You never got to the restaurant.

KARIN: No. "I have a headache."

(Then)

GEORGE: The buzzards are circling…

PATRICIA: What do you mean?

GEORGE: Where's my gun? *(To the buzzards)* 'We are not dead yet…'

PATRICIA: I don't understand.

JOYCE: *(Over this)* It's all right, Mom…

MARY: You'll have to eat with us, Karin…

KARIN: *(Getting up)* I can't do that. This is your—. It's a family thing. I know that… *(Then)* One year after Thomas' death…

HANNAH: Almost… It's tomorrow.

KARIN: *(To MARY)* You're the widow… I'll get something in town…

MARY: You're welcome to join us. Isn't she?

HANNAH: Stay.

JOYCE: *(Over this)* Of course.

MARY: Stay. Stay with us. And paint a cookie… We're all Gabriels.

KARIN: *(As she sits)* I just kept the name—. My agent said I shouldn't change it…

JOYCE: We just chose the shapes.

MARY: Get her some paper, George…

(GEORGE cuts another sheet of parchment paper.)

You want to change your dress?

KARIN: I'm fine. I 'll take off these…
(She takes off her heels.)

MARY: Where's Patricia's apron?

HANNAH: I put it back.

(HANNAH will get the apron and KARIN will put it on.)

JOYCE: *(Looking at GEORGE's work)* George has chosen Christmas trees.

GEORGE: They're autumn trees, Joyce. I'll paint them with fall foliage.

JOYCE: *(To GEORGE)* They'll look like lights. I think that cookie cutter is meant to be a Christmas tree—.

HANNAH: Leave him alone. They'll end up looking beautiful. Everything George touches ends up looking beautiful. He's an artist.

GEORGE: A craftsman.

HANNAH: That's an artist too.

MARY: *(To KARIN)* Here… [the parchment paper sheet]

JOYCE: Give her a couple of cookies.

HANNAH: Pick what you want.

(KARIN will put a couple of cut out cookies onto her parchment paper sheet.)

JOYCE: *(Half to herself)* Why didn't we make the Raggedy Ann Salad? That would have made my day... Aren't I easy to please, Mom...?
(She looks at PATRICIA, *who is asleep.)*
Mom's asleep.

(They all look at PATRICIA.*)*

HANNAH: *(To* KARIN*)* Let's not get your play script dirty...
(She moves it out of the way.)

KARIN: Oh I meant to show your mother these...
(Takes out glasses from her purse.)

JOYCE: What?

KARIN: Your Mother's glasses...

HANNAH: *(Same time)* Those were your Mother's...

(As KARIN *puts them on)*

HANNAH: *(Explains to* JOYCE*)* For Karin's show...

JOYCE: I know...

KARIN: She had glasses just like these. Young Hillary...
(Puts them away)

MARY: My daughter was fifteen when the whole Monica mess... I was visiting her and her Dad. *(To* KARIN*)* They're in Pittsburg. *(To all of them)* And she said about 'Monica and Bill': 'Oh, I'd never stay married to someone who cheated on me.' I know she meant to hurt me... I tried to explain—things are complicated. *(To* JOYCE*)* She's started calling more.

JOYCE: Good.

MARY: She's just feeling guilty...

(No one knows what to say.)

JOYCE: I can't believe that real estate guy, Karin. Your 'date'... Unbelievable.

KARIN: *(As a joke)* Well now everyone knows it wasn't a date.

GEORGE: *(Getting ready to paint)* The real estate agent handling Mom's house called me last Friday, Joyce. And says, he has potential clients who are visiting from the city, could he bring them around? I tell him, it's not even listed yet. And I hang up. Could you pass the red?

(JOYCE hands GEORGE the red paint.)

KARIN: I'll use this brush.

JOYCE: Don't ask. Just take it.

(KARIN takes the brush.)

GEORGE: He then calls right back and says he wishes to remind me of the fact that we don't actually own this house anymore. So he was just being polite and neighborly. And they'll be here in an hour. I explain we were busy. He says, he doesn't give a fuck. And 'please don't ever hang up on him again...' Could you hand me the green?

(Lights fade.)

6.
Done

(The same, a short time later.)

(GEORGE, HANNAH, JOYCE and KARIN paint cookies. MARY cuts vegetables for the salad. PATRICIA in a restless sleep.)

(In the middle of a conversation:)

JOYCE: *(Painting)* Why Kinderhook...?

KARIN: *(Half to herself, a joke)* 'Old Kinderhook': O K.

HANNAH: *(To* JOYCE, *over this)* Some very rich gallery owner from Manhattan bought their high school.

JOYCE: What??

MARY: I don't know about this. Why don't I know about this?

HANNAH: Their high school. Right in the middle of Kinderhook. I guess they'd built a new one? I don't know. I hope so. And completely renovated it.

GEORGE: *(Painting:)* Open one day a week.

JOYCE: How do they make any money—?

HANNAH: *(Over the end of this)* I don't think they have to, Joyce. *(Looks to* GEORGE*)* I don't understand either.

GEORGE: *(Painting:)* I don't know how those games are played...

HANNAH: *(To* MARY*)* I forgot to tell you. We saw this show by an African artist—Anatsui. I think that's how you say it. Do you know his stuff?

(Neither KARIN, JOYCE *nor* MARY *knows his work.)*

HANNAH: *(Explains)* He makes these giant—very colorful—

GEORGE: Beautiful—

HANNAH: —objects, most of them hang on a wall.

GEORGE: Out of thousands of little tiny bottle caps. All sewed together with wire.

HANNAH: They end up looking like magnificent tapestries. *(To* GEORGE*)* Don't they?

GEORGE: Incredible.

HANNAH: They flow... Then you get close and you see—it's all these found things.

GEORGE: All real stuff.

HANNAH: Then you step back again and it's— *(Looks to* GEORGE*)* —magnificent. Spiritual.

GEORGE: That's how we felt.

HANNAH: It made me happy just to be there. Among his whatever they are—in their presence.

JOYCE: *(To* GEORGE*)* From bottle caps?

*(*GEORGE *nods as he paints.)*

HANNAH: They just seem to be—and George and I said almost the same thing—overflowing with life. We kept thinking: they are living and breathing. And human. And real. These wired-together tiny bottle caps. You read on the wall that they are from liquor bottles; the sort imported into Africa from Europe… So I guess there's some 'dark' thing too: colonialism… *(Shrugs)*, yet out of that—from that—these things have been created, and they are beautiful. We were both just blown away.
(Then)
Then on the way out, there's a little room with some books, catalogues about the work, Anatsui's life… George picked up one—

GEORGE: And I happen to turn to one page where there's this 'intriguing' photograph… Of one of Anatsui's big pieces hanging in the lobby of the Bill and—whatshername Foundation.

HANNAH: I forget.

GEORGE: The Bill and whatshername Gates Foundation.

KARIN: I think it's M-something.

GEORGE: *(Over this)* And alongside the work on their lobby wall is a handsomely printed description about the making of it. It explains how village children in the artist's African town—.

HANNAH: And there's a little photograph of them –.

GEORGE: — how they help hammer the bottle caps
and tie them together with the wire. *And* for this the
artist, El Anatsui, repays their labor by sending them to
school.

JOYCE: Huh…

HANNAH: Obviously this is something this Foundation
wants to celebrate—trumpet—how through his
artwork this great artist gives back to his community,
by helping poor children go to school.

JOYCE: What's wrong with that? Sounds—

HANNAH: All this is explained in this catalogue. (*Puts
down her paintbrush*) And then it says that this isn't
true…

MARY: What isn't?

HANNAH: Someone at the Gates' Foundation seems to
have just made this all up.

JOYCE: What?

GEORGE: There's a photo in the catalogue of Anatsui
looking incredulous, maybe thinking: 'Where the hell
did they get his idea?' He doesn't pay for poor kids to
go school. It probably never even occurred to him to do
that. He pays them what he pays them, a going rate, for
where he lives and works; a rate we'd probably cringe
at, but that's what they get. They're paid to help him
make art. Which doesn't have to justify itself by quote
unquote doing something else.
(*Then*)
Just Art 'that shows or 'proves'—the capacity we,
human beings, have to create, out of our mess.' I'm
trying to quote him now. 'And while never denying
that the mess is there, we—by using just stuff, even
found stuff, bits of this and that, everyday normal stuff,
even if it's bottle caps—we celebrate being human.'

MARY: I like that, Hannah.

GEORGE: *(Over this)* But billionaires, we guessed, didn't we, Hannah? Must need to feel that they are buying more than just that. Things they can turn into something else.

(PATRICIA coughs in her sleep.)

KARIN: *(Noticing PATRICIA)* You think your mother's comfortable there?

(MARY goes to PATRICIA, and moves a blanket or pillow to make her more comfortable.)

JOYCE: Don't wake her up…. Please. I'm joking, Hannah…I'm so glad you finally got her wearing those things.

MARY: *(Over the end of this)* Depends.

JOYCE: Thank you for doing that.

GEORGE: Are you taking credit? It wasn't your idea.

HANNAH: *(Back to artists)* George told me a story about Alexander the Great and this great great artist.

GEORGE: You told me that it was sexist.

HANNAH: Not when I tell it. *(Continues)* What art can do as just art. What it shows. Allows us to see. Alexander commissions a portrait of his mistress. Then when he sees the painting finished, he realizes that this painter must appreciate her more and understand her better than he, Alexander, ever could. He sees that. He sees what he hasn't been seeing. So he just gives his mistress to the painter… *(To GEORGE)* That's the sexist part…

(Then)

MARY: A friend of mine, from Yale –. I don't know why that made me think of this. Ancient Greece I guess. She wrote Thomas maybe three, four days before he died.

JOYCE: So, like a year ago.

MARY: She's a Greek and Biblical scholar and she wanted to tell him about some new research into the New Testament. There's all sorts of electronic research now going on, she said. And so it's now being thought, that the word for the profession of St. Paul? I forget the Greek word. But forever it's been translated as 'tent-maker.' But now they think that's not what it really means.

HANNAH: You never told me this.

MARY: So I still have some secrets.

KARIN: What does it mean?

MARY: 'Prop maker.'

KARIN: You're kidding.

HANNAH: What???

MARY: 'Prop maker.' In a theater. The person who does the—props for a play. *(Picks up something off the table)* So it seems—that Saint Paul, the Saint Paul, got his start in theater!

(Smiles, shakes her head.)

HANNAH: Thomas must have loved that... Was he even able to hear that?

MARY: He always said theater and religion, they were like this... *(Fingers together)* I'm not sure I completely understood what he meant...

(JOYCE has paused from painting, and has picked up KARIN's manuscript of her 'play'.)

JOYCE: *(To KARIN)* Mind if I...?

KARIN: No... *(Explaining)* I jump from quote to quote. All her words. I've added nothing. *(Points)* Here... I like this... She's trying to find her feet again as First Lady. After that mess —

JOYCE: Which one?

KARIN: Health care… *(Explains)* At this point she's really lost.

GEORGE: Not for the first time and not the last.

JOYCE: *(Reads)* "…how best to make sure that children and families flourish…"

KARIN: I think she's trying to find her way back to that. The children. At this point.

JOYCE: In the early nineties.

KARIN: With health care.

GEORGE: I remember…

KARIN: To try and remember who the hell she really is…

HANNAH: So you think she keeps forgetting?

JOYCE: *(Reads)* "What we need is a new politics of Meaning…" That just sounds ridiculous now. *(Reads)* "…a society that fills us up again and makes us feel that we are a part of something bigger than ourselves…" Good luck. *(Reads)* "…coming off the last year when selfishness and greed…" "What does it mean to be educated? What does it mean in today's world to be human?" Ask him that. Ask him. Where is this Hillary now?

KARIN: Mostly from letters. Speeches…

HANNAH: Emails…?

KARIN: I love doing the moment when she's changing her name to Clinton… She both did and didn't want to do that. I understand that.

JOYCE: *(Continues, as she looks through the script)* "The séance"…? What séance?

KARIN: *(Explaining)* Her dark days in the White House, debilitating self-doubt…

JOYCE: I didn't know about this. Why don't I know about this? I thought we knew everything—

MARY: *(To* KARIN*)* You told me she was quite religious.

GEORGE: I didn't know that.

JOYCE: *(Reading, the 'séance')* Look who Hillary wanted to talk to: "Are you there, Eleanor Roosevelt?" "Eleanor, how did you, put up with all this?' She wanted to ask Eleanor that? *(Reads)* "Did you ever feel that you were carrying the history of womankind on your back?"

MARY: You think Eleanor answered her back?

JOYCE: *(Looks at* PATRICIA*)* Mom told me on the phone this week that she'd voted twice for Eleanor Roosevelt. 'No, you didn't, Mom. She didn't run for anything...'

HANNAH: May I see? *(To* KARIN*)* Do you mind?

*(*JOYCE *hands* HANNAH *the manuscript.)*

JOYCE: I went back to Val Kill recently.

HANNAH: When did you—?

JOYCE: Six, seven weeks ago? After coming here. When I came up to see Mom, after the stroke. A friend met me there.

GEORGE: What friend?

JOYCE: She'd never been. She lives over in New Paltz, but she'd never been to Val Kill. Anyway, you know Hillary's photograph is all over...

KARIN: *(Over the end of this)* She loves Val Kill. I was just going to say that.

JOYCE: *(Over this)* My friend and I—.

HANNAH: Who is she?

JOYCE: We were in the little gift shop. We were the only two in there except for the lady behind the counter. My friend asks if the planks out there on the lawn were where the swimming pool used to be. The woman explains that the first pool was on the other side of the house. 'Why are you ladies interested in the pool?' she asks. My friend says she's just curious about Eleanor's friends, the women who lived here with her. The couples. This woman, she looks at the two of us, obviously she sees there is no one else in the shop; she then lifts out from under the counter a kind of scrapbook of photos: 'Here,' she says. 'Look here...' And she opens it up.

(Then)

There are all these black and white photographs of Eleanor—in her bathing suit. By the pool laughing. Her arm around one woman. Both of them are laughing. Just being... I suppose—herself. Allowing herself to be herself...

HANNAH: Did you tell your Mom that?

JOYCE: About Eleanor?

HANNAH: Everything, Joyce. Visiting there with a friend...

JOYCE: Why would I?

HANNAH: You should.

JOYCE: I don't think she'd be interested...

HANNAH: Don't just assume.

(They paint.)

MARY: Your Mom and I went to a séance.

JOYCE: Why would you—?

KARIN: *(Same time)* I don't know about— *(This)*

MARY: *(Over this)* I think she remembers going.... It was her idea. Some place on Long Island. You pay six hundred dollars—.

JOYCE: When was—?

HANNAH: Last winter.

MARY: We didn't know we were broke then. We'd read about it in *The Times.* How—even being around other people 'pretending'. How that could be helpful. And so we went to try and talk with Thomas.

(GEORGE *looks at* HANNAH.)

HANNAH: I didn't tell you, George.

MARY: A Mr Edward was the medium; he called himself something else. There were seven of us. Each one of us, I guess, just wasn't ready to let go of someone...

JOYCE: Did you talk to Thomas?

MARY: (*Smiles*) No. Of course not. (*Looks at* PATRICIA) It was in his basement rec room. Golf trophies in the bookcase. A folded-up ping pong table. But there was something in it though, that we all needed...

JOYCE: What?

MARY: I suppose: to accept that it was okay to not want to just cut it off. Accept that it can and maybe even should be a long journey. Not to try too hard to 'move on' —rather, when things are really hard, you can tell yourself, it was okay just to 'move.'
(*Then*)
(*Changing the subject*) It's election day. We should be talking about that, shouldn't we?

HANNAH: Paulie's first time.

JOYCE: (*To* GEORGE) So Paulie was excited voting. Hannah said he was like a kid.

GEORGE: (*Smiling*) But holding his nose. Just before he went behind the voting desk, he turned to me and held his nose. Like a kid.

HANNAH: It was a joke.

GEORGE: When we were walking out of the Town Hall, Hannah, he said to me, "Dad, it could have been about so much more..."

HANNAH: Sorry, son. They're usually not like this.

MARY: We're better than this, Paulie.

JOYCE: We sure about that?

GEORGE: "I thought I'd be inspired, Dad. Not just scared."

KARIN: He said that?

JOYCE: *(Same time)* Wrong election.

(Then)

GEORGE: My first time voting. Like Paulie, I'd come back from college just for the day. My Dad wanted me to go with him and for some reason we'd waited until around about this time at night, so it was dark out... And a beautiful Fall night. Like tonight. The crunch of leaves under our feet; the Dutch Reform's church bells. The town hall lit up. Dad said to me, 'Everyone should have his first experience voting for Jimmy Carter—in Rhinebeck'. Dad...

HANNAH: The first time I voted...

GEORGE: Where were you— *(Living)*?

HANNAH: Pine Plains then.

GEORGE: Right. With that guy with really long— *(Gestures: sideburns)*

HANNAH: *(Ignoring him)* I got Mondale...I finished, pulled that lever to open the curtain, and suddenly thought—did I do it right?

GEORGE: What do you mean?

HANNAH: *(Over this)* Did I make a mistake?

GEORGE: What choice did you have?

JOYCE: *(Over this)* I often think that, Hannah.

HANNAH: I mean, George, did I miss voting for some question? I remembered there were going to be questions, but I didn't see them. Later, my mom asked me if I'd voted yes on some—very very important question. I felt like I'd fucked up...

GEORGE: Because you fucked up.

MARY: I was visiting my daughter; they'd just moved away to Pittsburg, to my ex's family. This isn't about a first time, but about an election day. And I'm staying in a motel. She was allowed to come over and stay one night with me. I'd completely forgotten it was election day. That happens. I'm sure that happens to a lot of people when you're overwhelmed...I turned the T V on; there were the results. We're lying each in our twin bed...Natalie Merchant starts to sing... And we then see the two of them walk out holding hands. This is of course in Little Rock.
(Then)
My daughter says all excited: 'Oh she looks so beautiful...' I look at my daughter in her bed, and I say, 'She's the wife..." I reminded her of that last night when she called, Hannah.

HANNAH: Did she remember?

MARY: She did. I was surprised. *(Then)* I said—'well, now she's not just the wife...'
(Then)

GEORGE: *(To KARIN)* Natalie Merchant lives in Rhinebeck.

KARIN: Does she?

HANNAH: We've seen her two, three times in the health food store. I think she moved.

MARY: Can I paint a cookie…? I want to paint one cookie…

HANNAH: *(Over the end of this)* Of course… Why are you asking…?

JOYCE: *(Same time)* Mary. Give her a brush.

HANNAH: Get her a cookie…

GEORGE: One left.

KARIN: Take a paintbrush…

(MARY *sits and joins them.)*

HANNAH: By now Faso and Teachout together have spent thirteen, fourteen million dollars to win our little rural district.

MARY: I read that too in *The Freeman.*

HANNAH: And nearly all of that—both sides—they say, has come from people who don't live here. This morning, I left that circle empty…

(Then)

KARIN: In my show I want people to see Hillary, the person… One of the women who invited me… She kept saying: 'Tonight, just do the nice parts. Only the nice parts…'

MARY: Just her better angels…

KARIN: Right.

MARY: A friend wrote me the other day; she lives in Chicago. She said there's a billboard in one of those really tough neighborhoods on the South Side—.

GEORGE: Where all those kids are being killed—.

MARY: Yeh. And it says: 'Your ticket out of here.' It's for the state lottery. The Illinois State Lottery. My friend wrote: 'See, Mr Trump, he's not alone. What have we become?' Who are we? 'Who's there?'

(Smiles)

JOYCE: *(To* HANNAH*)* Careful… You're dripping…
[on Karin's manuscript. Then picking up the script, to
KARIN) I'll put this over on the bench, Karin… Get it
out of the way…
(She will set the script on the bench and sit there, watching
PATRICIA.*)*

KARIN: Good idea. Thanks.

*(*PATRICIA *mumbles in her sleep.)*

JOYCE: Mom's dreaming… *(Looking at* PATRICIA*)*
George, did you hear what she said?
'I wanted more than that for you.' More than what?

GEORGE: I don't know….

MARY: *(As she paints)* Ever feel like this? I take a
shower, and all I'm thinking—is I'll be over with that
soon. Then I have breakfast, while I'm thinking: what's
next? I'm putting on my face—getting that over with.
Check. Check mark. Over with that. Done with that.

(Timer goes off)

MARY: What now? Now What?

(Then)

HANNAH: Your timer…

MARY: I know. Dinner. Someone should set the table.

GEORGE: I can do that…

JOYCE: *(Having noticed a notebook on the bench)* Listen
to this. I just saw this… This is one of Thomas'
notebooks?

MARY: Shit, leave that in the basket.

GEORGE: *(Surprised)* Mary?

HANNAH: *(Over this)* What is it?

JOYCE: *(Ignoring her)* He's written here: "A play where everyone is always cooking."

KARIN: We read that.

MARY: Joyce, just give that to me…
(Reaches out for it.)

KARIN: Hold on, Joyce… There's something else in that notebook.

MARY: Karin. Give it to me…

JOYCE: What?

KARIN: Mary, show them what we did in that notebook yesterday.

JOYCE: What? Why is it in here?

KARIN: I'll show you. Let me have it.

MARY: *(As JOYCE starts to give it to KARIN)* Don't give it to her.

HANNAH: What's this about?

MARY: *(Over this)* Karin, they don't need to see—.

HANNAH: See what?

MARY: Joyce!

HANNAH: *(Over this)* Mary, I've never seen you like this.

KARIN: *(Same time, to JOYCE)* Give it here. *(Taking the notebook and going through it)* I think they do, Mary. I think they'd be really interested in this…

JOYCE: Mary's blushing… I'm interested. Why are you blushing?

HANNAH: *(Smiling)* I don't know anything about this.

MARY: It's not funny. Fuck you…

(To GEORGE who has stopped to watch)

MARY: I thought you were going to set the table.

GEORGE: I'm interested.

MARY: Damn it, give that to me, Karin—!

KARIN: No! We wrote something— *(Corrects herself)* re-*wrote* something—.

GEORGE: In Thomas' notebook?

KARIN: In this one. *(To* MARY*)* Didn't we? What did we write—?

MARY: *(Over this)* George, tell her to give me back the notebook.

*(*GEORGE *ignores* MARY.*)*

MARY: Dinner's ready.
(She will take the Shepherd's Pie out of the oven as:)

KARIN: *(Finding the page in the notebook)* Here it is. It's a monologue. We just came across this, didn't we? *(Holds it up)* He'd written the whole thing out. *(To* MARY*)* Right? Come on, it's funny. *(To the others)* Mary said he used to do that, as notes for a play. To use later... We've come across a bunch of them. Different people. This one...
(Looks at MARY*)*

JOYCE: What?

KARIN: This one...

*(*KARIN *holds the notebook out to* MARY*, she doesn't try to grab it.)*

KARIN: You want to explain?

*(*MARY *busies herself with the peas.)*

KARIN: We just happened across it. It's about a...

JOYCE: What?

KARIN: A female doctor...

EVERYONE: *(Interested)* Oh! Mary...

JOYCE: *(Over this)* About Mary. Something Thomas wrote.

GEORGE: What about Mary?

KARIN: *(Over this)* Her same age. The doctor here. Exactly Mary's age when he wrote it. We figured that out, didn't we? He wrote in the dates… Anyway, so 'Vi' —he calls her 'Vi', the doctor. She—*you* want to tell them? *(Continues)* She comes home from work one day, from her practice, wearing a—what? A brown pants suit. And a pretty much non-descript—his words— grey sweater.

MARY: It's not really grey. And I don't know why it's 'non-descript'.

KARIN: She knew the sweater…

MARY: It's very comfortable.

KARIN: And 'Vi' throws herself into a chair—*that* seems to be the set—one chair—and begins to—what? Complain? Worry? She's been shaken up by something at work.

MARY: She's not complaining.

KARIN: *(Over this)* You told me you'd said some of these exact things. About—feeling hopeless.

MARY: Not always. Sometimes.

KARIN: *(Over this)* Impotent. Being—a doctor. In this— that very day, she'd seen one of her patients die.

MARY: I think he was trying to turn her into one of those Russian doctors—in the plays he loves so much. Full of frustrations—.

KARIN: Mary—. I read it to Mary. And she says, 'let me see that…' And she takes a pencil and begins crossing things out—

GEORGE: In his notebook?

KARIN: And adding things. What did you add? Tell them….

MARY: We cut the pants suit. That was the first thing we cut.

KARIN: *(Reads)* "Vi" now "enters, having changed from her drab doctor's work clothes into… a 'powder blue silk dressing gown with a sweet butterfly pattern,' Where online did we see that? We researched…

GEORGE: I can't believe this—.

HANNAH: When did you do this?

KARIN: *(Holding up the notebook)* She *(MARY)* wrote all over it… *(Reads)* "That catches all the lovely curves of her exquisite body…"

HANNAH: What website?

MARY: *(To KARIN)* You added that. We crossed out stuff too. *(Answering HANNAH)* Way beyond J Crew, Hannah. Way beyond your imagination.

HANNAH: What the fuck does that mean?

MARY: *(To HANNAH)* You should shop online with Karin sometime.

KARIN: And we put her into some very nice pajamas. I'd like to have those pajamas. And then here as she's beginning to talk—she makes herself a cocktail.

MARY: *(To KARIN)* Karin knows the names of all these fancy cocktails… What did we decide?

KARIN: *(Over the end of this)* We hadn't made a final choice. We were testing…

MARY: *(To HANNAH)* I don't know how she knows them.

HANNAH: Were you both drunk? Was this at night?

KARIN: *(Paraphrasing)* Mary has a cocktail—*(Corrects herself)* Vi has a cocktail in hand. *(To HANNAH) middle* of the day. *(Continues)* She is *not*—*no longer*—sitting on a chair, but now she sits on a *divan.*

MARY: I always wanted a divan. Thomas said they're 'too pretentious…'

KARIN: *(Continues)* And she leans back on the divan… And this was a nice touch. Whose idea was this? *(Shrugs)* "As she begins to calmly talk to us—"

MARY: I added 'calmly.' What did he write?

KARIN: We crossed it out. I can't read it. *(Continues)* "One hears the soft sensual rustle of her nylons as she crosses her legs…"

(Phone rings off.)

JOYCE & HANNAH: Phone…

GEORGE: I got it.

HANNAH: *(To GEORGE)* Maybe it's Paulie.

GEORGE: *(To MARY and KARIN)* I can't believe you two did that…
(He heads off.)

JOYCE: I thought she had pajamas on.

MARY: What do you mean?

JOYCE: *(Over the end of this)* Then why is she wearing nylons?

MARY: *(To KARIN)* We need to change that.

HANNAH: *(To MARY)* That is so unlike you. It's childish…

KARIN: We know.

MARY: I know. But he's not here, Hannah. So fuck him. He shouldn't have died.

(At first no one knows how to respond, then she smiles.)

HANNAH: Then I guess it serves him right...? Can I see? Fuck him...

(Then)

KARIN: There's almost nothing left of the thing Thomas wrote... We spent like what? Like five hours on it.

MARY: Give me that.
(She takes the notebook:)
(Speaks to the notebook) She doesn't just complain. She isn't always unhappy. She's fucking sexy. And she's hopeful. And she's getting on with her goddamn life!
(She puts the notebook back on the bench, then to the notebook:)
Or she will.
(Then)
Let's have dinner. George was supposed to set the table...

KARIN: I can do that, Mary. I'll do that...
(She heads off to the dining room.)

JOYCE: Does she know which plates to use?

MARY: She knows...

JOYCE: *(Calls)* The white plates...

MARY: *(Over this)* She knows. I just want to finish painting my damn cookie...Joyce, you better wake up your mother.
(She sits and paints her cookie.)

(JOYCE has sat and looks at PATRICIA:*)*

JOYCE: You know I almost forgot Mom was here.
No, I didn't. Mom...today I kept hearing your voice...

HANNAH: I thought that was just your stomach...

JOYCE: You do sound like my stomach... Hearing you say: 'We're putting on a show.' *(To* MARY*)* I think because of the stuff you've been digging through. I remembered this… She used to do for my birthdays—wonderful puppet shows. Did you know that?

(MARY *shakes her head.*)

HANNAH: I remember those.

JOYCE: Down in the rec room. She'd ring a bell: 'We're putting on a show.' Someone could be crying, or fighting. And that was her answer to everything: 'We're putting on a show.' All my friends thought you were so amazing…

HANNAH: I know I did…

JOYCE: *(Gently waking up* PATRICIA*)* Mom? Hi… Mom? Hello? Hi… We're having dinner… Wake up….

PATRICIA: *(Waking up)* What…??

JOYCE: *(At the same time)* You were asleep.

PATRICIA: What?

JOYCE: I think you were voting for Eleanor Roosevelt. Mom, someone's just phoned. *(After a look at the others)* Can you tell us—who's on the phone? Use your magical powers.

HANNAH: Joyce…

PATRICIA: What…? I wasn't asleep.

JOYCE: Who's on the phone, Mom? Come on, you always know…. And I've always found that really creepy. Is it Paulie? We think it's Paulie.

HANNAH: *(To* JOYCE*)* Your Mom's wheelchair, it's… [points by the sink]

(JOYCE *looks at* HANNAH.)

HANNAH: Will you do it?

(JOYCE *looks at* MARY.)

MARY: *(Painting)* I'm busy, Joyce.

JOYCE: *(Getting the wheelchair)* Who is it, Mom? Is it Paulie?

PATRICIA: *(Half asleep)* It's Paulie.

JOYCE: *(To HANNAH as 'fact')* It's your son. He's on the phone.

PATRICIA: *(To JOYCE)* It's Paulie…

JOYCE: We know, Mom. We know. You always know… *(About the wheelchair)* Mary, how do you open this up?

MARY: Figure it out.

HANNAH: You need to learn…

(JOYCE looks to HANNAH.)

HANNAH: The handles…

JOYCE: Why are you doing this?

MARY: *(Painting)* Doing what?

HANNAH: I'll take the salad, Mary. And see how Karin's doing…

(They see GEORGE returning; HANNAH stops.)

HANNAH: Was it Paulie?

GEORGE: No, Karin's date.

(JOYCE looks at PATRICIA.)

JOYCE: Mom…

PATRICIA: What, Joyce?

HANNAH: *(Over this)* Calling to apologize…?

MARY: Fuck him. *(To HANNAH)* I'm on a roll.

GEORGE: He wanted to know how far back the property goes…

(HANNAH heads off with the salad bowl.)

GEORGE: How can I help?

MARY: Karin is setting the table.

JOYCE: *(Still with the folded up wheelchair)* George, how do you do this?

MARY: Let her do it, George. She'll work it out.

GEORGE: Are we drinking wine?

MARY: We don't want wine, do we?

GEORGE: We might need it…

(JOYCE opens the wheelchair.)

MARY: See. She did it. Good for you, Joyce.

JOYCE: Here we go, Mom…

GEORGE: Put the brakes on…

JOYCE: Where are the brakes?

GEORGE: Those things right there.

JOYCE: This?
(She puts the brakes on.)

(KARIN returns.)

KARIN: *(To MARY)* We're doing a tablecloth or placemats? I set out placemats. Hannah thinks we should have a tablecloth. Mary, if you want a tablecloth…

MARY: Placemats are fine. It doesn't matter….

JOYCE: *(To PATRICIA)* Okay, Mom?

(All watch JOYCE:)

JOYCE: Put your arm…Mom…

GEORGE: She can't move that arm, Joyce.
(He will get a pitcher of water out of the refrigerator, and refill it.)

JOYCE: I know!

MARY: *(Still painting, before GEORGE can help)* They're doing fine. Let them…

JOYCE: *(To* PATRICIA*)* Put your arm, that arm, Mom.
Here.

(As they watch:)

JOYCE: *(As she gets ready to help up her mother)* I've been
wanting to ask you, George, what did the guy from
New York think about the house? Who came to see
it last week. He did come, right? I'm just curious. *(To*
PATRICIA*)* Ready?

GEORGE: He said it was too small.

*(*PATRICIA *loses her grip on* JOYCE:*)*

JOYCE: It's okay. *(To the others)* We're fine.

*(*HANNAH *has returned; she will strain the peas in the sink,
and put them in a bowl.)*

GEORGE: *(Back to the house)* I heard him ask if the house
could be knocked down...

PATRICIA: Knocked down?
(She looks up at JOYCE.*)*

JOYCE: We don't own it, Mom.

GEORGE: *(Continuing)* I guess so he could build
something bigger...

JOYCE: *(To* PATRICIA*)* One more time. Ready...? Good.
Good. There. Good. You're in... Are you in?

*(*PATRICIA *is in the wheelchair.)*

JOYCE: There you go... *(To the others)* I did it. I'll take
you into the dining room.... *(A bad joke)* Fasten your
seatbelt...I know, you're not a child. It's a joke, Mom.
(To others) I'll sit with Mom, keep her company. Please
don't be too long.

(As they go:)

JOYCE: You want to sit at the table in your wheelchair
or in a grown-up chair? I'm teasing you, Mom... Don't
be long.

(They are gone.)

GEORGE: *(About* JOYCE *and* PATRICIA*)* Let's give them about—a half an hour alone together…

*(*KARIN*, getting out silverware:)*

KARIN: I thought the Village was an historic district, so you can't just knock things down….

GEORGE: They get around that. Just let a property go to hell… They let you knock it down then.

MARY: It's not right…

GEORGE: What does 'right' have to do with anything? *(With the water pitcher)* I'll set out water glasses… *(He goes off.)*

HANNAH: *(To* KARIN*)* The Church across the street did that with a house… Just let it go… The church. Karin, can you also take the peas?

KARIN: My mother used to always say, "Pray for peace and spiritual food and for wisdom and guidance, for all these are good. But don't forget the potatoes…" *(Looking at the Shepherd's Pie)* Smells good, Mary.

*(*KARIN *goes off with the silverware and the peas.)*

HANNAH: *(To* MARY*)* I put on a tablecloth… Are we still taking Patricia to vote…?

MARY: If there's time… Is there time?

HANNAH: I think she's forgotten about it…

MARY: *(Shrugs)* She's going to win. The other is unthinkable.

HANNAH: And if she doesn't?

MARY: Maybe we just follow the crowds to the cliff, Hannah, hold hands, and jump. Shouting 'what about us?? We should probably ask Patricia, let her decide. There's still time…

(HANNAH *has gone to get napkins out of the table drawer.*)

HANNAH: Karin was just telling me that she's now thinking of moving on Friday. I guess she's in a hurry...

MARY: Just one day sooner. She doesn't teach on Fridays...Kingston's nice...

HANNAH: I'll get George to help Karin.

MARY: She doesn't have much stuff...

HANNAH: What cookie did you choose?

MARY: I didn't choose anything. The only one left. A person. But I'm giving her a nice big smile, Hannah...

HANNAH: I think Uptown Kingston does kind of feel how Rhinebeck used to. You know what I mean? It's only the people who live there. That's nice.

MARY: It is.

HANNAH: George was telling me that just a few doors down from Karin's new apartment—not the lawyers out of Dickens, in the other direction, is the house where John Wilkes Booth's brother, the famous actor, where he hid out, after his brother had shot Lincoln. He came and stayed, and I guess felt safe there. (*The joke*) George said—see, even then no one went to Kingston...
(*Smiles*)

MARY: That's funny...Hannah. "Things do work out... That's what we have to keep telling ourselves, damn it."

HANNAH: Thomas?

MARY: Yeh.

(HANNAH *goes off to the dining room, with the napkins.*)

(MARY *has finished her cookie and begins to collect the others onto a cookie sheet. Piano music from the living room: Schumann's album Pour La Jeunesse, No. 6, Armes Waisenkind.)*

(She sits and listens to the music.)

(HANNAH returns.)

MARY: What do you need?

(HANNAH goes to the refrigerator.)

HANNAH: George wants wine. I saw an open bottle of white…I'll smell it…Joyce doesn't like my salad dressing. She wants the Paul Newman. I'll call Paulie after we eat. *(The wine)* Smells fine. Patricia wants a pillow for her back…
(She goes to pick up a pillow from a chair.)

MARY: Hannah, we did sell the piano, didn't we? And they took it away…?

(HANNAH just looks at MARY.)

MARY: I still hear him… Even after a year… He used to play this to me… *(Obviously)* You can't hear it.

(HANNAH shakes her head.)

HANNAH: No. What are you going to do?

(Then)

MARY: I've finished my cookie. I'm gathering the others. I'll put them in the oven. Then set the timer. Remind me, we might not hear it in the dining room. Then I'll bring in the Shepherd's Pie. We'll have dinner… I've got it all planned out, Hannah.
(Smiles)
I'll be right there.

(HANNAH goes.)

(MARY continues to collect the cookies and listen to the short piano piece. It finishes. after a moment:)

MARY: You done?

(Silence)

(As MARY *puts the cookies in the oven and sets the timer:)*

(Music: Lucius' Until We Get There *from the theater speakers. she looks over the table and the room, puts on oven mitts, picks up the Shepherd's Pie; after one more look across the kitchen, the table, she goes to join the others in the diningroom.)*

(Blackout)

END OF PLAY

NOTE

I consulted and read the following books while writing
WOMEN OF A CERTAIN AGE: Carl Bernstein's *A
Woman in Charge*; Dick Morris' *Behind the Oval Office*;
Peter Ackroyd's *The English Ghost Story*; Matt Taibbi's
The Divide; Sheila Heti, Heidi Julavits & Leanne
Shapton's *Women in Clothes*; M F K Fischer's *The Art of
Eating*; Brillat-Savarin's *The Physiology of Taste*; Anne
Hollander's *Feeding the Eye*; *Olivier Assayas* (edited by
Kent Jones); Alice Munro's *Runaway*; Oliver Sacks' *On
The Move* and *Hallucinations*; W G Sebald's *The Rings of
Saturn*; Laurie Colwin's *Home Cooking*; Claire Bidwell
Smith's article in *The New York Times* about visiting a
psychic.

The *Ladies Home Journal* which Joyce reads from is
issue September 1, 1910; the cookbook they use is
Betty Crocker's Cook Book for Boys and Girls (1957); the
songbook is Opal Wheeler's *Sing for America (1944)*; the
story about Edwin Booth comes from Jervis McEntee
(published by The Friends of Historic Kingston); the
discovery about Saint Paul's life in the theater comes
from my friend Larissa; the 'ice-breaker' comes from
Jocelyn.

WOMEN OF A CERTAIN AGE is a play and a work
of fiction, and it is not based upon any living person or
persons.

R N, Rhinebeck.

www.ingramcontent.com/pod-product-compliance
Lightning Source LLC
Chambersburg PA
CBHW070018110426
42741CB00034B/2154